**New Directions for
Community Colleges**

Arthur M. Cohen
EDITOR-IN-CHIEF

Florence B. Brawer
ASSOCIATE EDITOR

Carrie B. Kisker
MANAGING EDITOR

Academic Pathways To and From the Community College

Debra D. Bragg
Elisabeth A. Barnett
EDITORS

Number 135 • Fall 2006
Jossey-Bass
San Francisco

ACADEMIC PATHWAYS TO AND FROM THE COMMUNITY COLLEGE
Debra D. Bragg, Elisabeth A. Barnett (eds.)
New Directions for Community Colleges, no. 135

Arthur M. Cohen, Editor-in-Chief
Florence B. Brawer, Associate Editor

NEW DIRECTIONS FOR COMMUNITY COLLEGES (ISSN 0194-3081, electronic ISSN 1536-0733) is part of The Jossey-Bass Higher and Adult Education Series and is published quarterly by Wiley Subscription Services, Inc., A Wiley Company, at Jossey-Bass, 989 Market Street, San Francisco, California 94103-1741. Periodicals Postage Paid at San Francisco, California, and at additional mailing offices. POSTMASTER: Send address changes to New Directions for Community Colleges, Jossey-Bass, 989 Market Street, San Francisco, California 94103-1741.

SUBSCRIPTIONS cost $80.00 for individuals and $195.00 for institutions, agencies, and libraries. Prices subject to change. See order form at the back of book.

EDITORIAL CORRESPONDENCE should be sent to the Editor-in-Chief, Arthur M. Cohen, at the Graduate School of Education and Information Studies, University of California, Box 951521, Los Angeles, California 90095-1521. All manuscripts receive anonymous reviews by external referees.

New Directions for Community Colleges is indexed in Current Index to Journals in Education (ERIC).

Microfilm copies of issues and articles are available in 16mm and 35mm, as well as microfiche in 105mm, through University Microfilms Inc., 300 North Zeeb Road, Ann Arbor, Michigan 48106-1346.

CONTENTS

EDITORS' NOTES

Nearly all youths in the United States desire a college education, yet for many, the gap between high school and college remains disturbingly wide. Past policies and practices have not gone far enough to create academic pathways that lead from high school to college or enable transfer from two- to four-year colleges and universities. In particular, minority, low-income, first-generation, and other K–12 students labeled the *forgotten half* or the *neglected majority* are less likely than their white and more affluent peers to realize their dream of going to college. As a result, educational and economic outcomes associated with academic achievement and college attendance are distributed inequitably among youth in the United States. Without interventions that dramatically change curricula, instruction, assessment, and infrastructure, this situation will not change. In fact, we argue it will likely worsen.

For several decades, community colleges have played a leading role in facilitating students' transitions from secondary to postsecondary education, and through completion of the baccalaureate degree. Yet better policies, models, and programs are needed if all students are to successfully complete their educational goals. Through state and federal policy, emerging local structures, and collaborative partnerships at all levels, academic pathway models are connecting high schools to community colleges and community colleges to universities in order to meet the needs of students who have not traditionally participated in higher education.

This volume of *New Directions for Community Colleges* looks at developments in local, state, and federal policies and programs designed to enhance opportunities for more students—especially those traditionally underserved in higher education—to access and succeed in college, paying particular attention to the role of community colleges in this process. We look at secondary curricular and organizational restructuring that is occurring in collaboration with postsecondary institutions, particularly curricular reforms designed to help students perform at higher academic levels and prepare them to transition to college ready to learn. Chapter authors discuss dual credit, dual enrollment, and early and middle college high schools, as well as initiatives that aim to enhance college access by integrating academic and career or technical subjects. To varying degrees, each of these models has played a role in reaching out to underserved student populations.

Chapter One, by Debra Bragg, Eunyoung Kim, and Elisabeth Barnett, reports the results of a fifty-state research and development project funded by the Lumina Foundation for Education called Academic Pathways to Access and Student Success (APASS). The chapter also presents information

NEW DIRECTIONS FOR COMMUNITY COLLEGES, no. 135, Fall 2006 © Wiley Periodicals, Inc.
Published online in Wiley InterScience (www.interscience.wiley.com) • DOI: 10.1002/cc.242

about new and emerging academic pathways that systematically link high schools to two- and four-year colleges and enhance access for students traditionally underserved in higher education. By articulating the issues that undergird the APASS project, as well as the goals and outcomes of many other initiatives described in this volume, we strive to deepen understanding of models and approaches that link high school to college and address the needs of underserved students.

Subsequent chapters offer insight into various dimensions of the pathways linking high school to college. In Chapter Two, Denise Green describes what we know about traditionally underserved students, including students of color, first-generation students, and low-income students. She discusses how they fare in college transitions and what educators still need to know to effectively serve them. Chapter Three, written by Andrea Bueschel and Andrea Venezia, describes examples of local pathways and statewide policies that align community college standards and curricula with those at high schools and four-year colleges and universities.

In Chapter Four, Erika Hunt and Charles Carroll present a case study of one of the nation's oldest dual enrollment programs: Florida's Accelerated Mechanism Program. Through a discussion of the development of the state's policies governing dual enrollment and an intensive look at one Florida community college, this chapter identifies successful strategies, challenges, and barriers in implementing a P–16 academic pathway. Chapter Five spotlights early and middle college high schools, and explains how students can graduate with a high school diploma and an associate degree after five years. In this chapter, Terry Born describes the development of two such schools, with particular emphasis on how they support students taking college-level courses while still in high school. Chapter Six shifts the discussion of academic pathways to the intersection of community colleges and four-year institutions. In this chapter, Deborah Floyd identifies the different ways in which community colleges participate in baccalaureate education and debunks myths surrounding the controversial community college baccalaureate degree.

The following three chapters provide insight into how traditional career and workforce curricula are being aligned with rigorous academic instruction to enhance access to college for students who have traditionally forgone college to enter the workforce. In Chapter Seven, Donna Dare discusses recent attempts to promote students' transitions into postsecondary education through reforms associated with career and technical education. In Chapter Eight, Margaret Ann Draeger highlights a high-tech partnership led by a Tech Prep consortium that involves high schools, a community college, and neighboring universities in Ohio. Chapter Nine, written by Cheri St. Arnauld, describes the way community college, business, and government partners have created an accessible teacher education pathway for students in Arizona. Finally, Chapter Ten, written by Elisabeth Barnett and Debra Bragg, synthesizes the previous chapters and discusses lessons learned and promising policies and practices in creating and sustaining academic pathways to and from the community college.

Debra D. Bragg
Elisabeth A. Barnett
Editors

DEBRA D. BRAGG *is professor of higher education and community college leadership, and director of the APASS initiative at the University of Illinois at Urbana-Champaign.*

ELISABETH A. BARNETT *is senior research associate with the National Center for Restructuring Education, Schools, and Teaching at Teachers College, Columbia University, in New York, and a former APASS team member.*

NEW DIRECTIONS FOR COMMUNITY COLLEGES • DOI: 10.1002/cc

1

This chapter discusses results of a fifty-state study conducted through the Academic Pathways to Access and Student Success initiative, and identifies curricular, instructional, and organizational approaches that increase opportunities for underserved students to attend college.

Creating Access and Success: Academic Pathways Reaching Underserved Students

Debra D. Bragg, Eunyoung Kim, Elisabeth A. Barnett

The aspiration to attend college is nearly universal among American youth, yet the fulfillment of such desires is much more limited. According to the U.S. Department of Education (2004), roughly 90 percent of the 2002 high school sophomore cohort desired a college education, and over 70 percent expected to complete a four-year college degree. In actuality, only 62 percent of this group enrolled in college, and nearly half of the college entrants failed to return for a second year. Those who do not enter or remain in college do not experience the same benefits, such as increased annual earnings, as college graduates (Howe, 1988; Rosenbaum, 2001).

The term *college access* links a number of different issues: how low- and middle-income families pay college costs, how students traditionally underrepresented in higher education overcome discrimination and social disadvantage, and how well high school graduates are prepared for college-level work (Cabrera and La Nasa, 2001). Several researchers and policymakers have addressed the importance of curricular and institutional structures that enhance links between secondary and postsecondary education (Lee, Smith,

Funding for this work was provided by the Lumina Foundation for Education through a grant to the Office of Community College Research and Leadership at the University of Illinois at Urbana-Champaign for the Academic Pathways to Access and Student Success initiative.

and Croninger, 1995; Lewis, 2003). Nonetheless, greater efforts to increase access to and success in college through enhanced alignment and improved curricula do not necessarily translate into successful outcomes for underserved students. Success in college depends on their having adequate academic preparation so they can be retained in college and earn credentials. Initiatives that bridge the curricular gap between high school and college are often partially implemented or underutilized, partly because of insufficient government financial support or inadequate institutional capacity and commitment (Lee and Bryk, 1988).

Academic Pathways

Pathways are one way of thinking about secondary-to-postsecondary transition opportunities; academic pathways refer to boundary-spanning curricula, instructional and organizational strategies, and meaningful assessments that either link or extend from high school to college, including both two- and four-year institutions. Academic pathways support student transition by straddling secondary and postsecondary education, helping students overcome hurdles or fill in gaps that would otherwise stand in their way. They often involve new organizational structures or policy mechanisms that are designed to integrate different levels of education.

A number of different models and approaches to the transition from high school to college are proliferating throughout the United States. These initiatives are either expanding on old ideas or creating new ones to support student matriculation to college. Some of these models explicitly aim to enhance access to college for students who have been historically underrepresented in higher education. These academic pathways encourage students who are likely to face barriers to college entry and attendance to engage in advanced learning in academic- and career-related subjects at the K–12 level and provide support structures to ease their transition to college. This chapter's discussion is organized into three sections: the community college role in academic pathways, academic pathway initiatives to support access and student success, and finally, results of a nationwide study of these programs: the Academic Pathways to Student Success (APASS) initiative. The discussion of APASS results includes information about whether states—or localities within states—make special efforts to reach underserved students, and whether the academic pathways have legislative support. We conclude by considering the limitations and future potential of academic pathways for increasing college access.

The Role of the Community College in Academic Pathways

Community colleges play an important role in expanding access to college by enrolling students who are members of ethnic minority groups or who are low income, first generation, or underprepared for college-level work. In 2003, for example, students of color represented 36 percent of all students enrolled in community colleges (U.S. Department of Education, 2005). As well, recent research (Kurlaender, 2006) has shown that for Latinos, community colleges are the higher education institution of choice. Because of their open access mission and state and local governing bodies that are similar to—and sometimes the same as—those for K–12 schools, community colleges are often better suited to work with both K–12 schools and other community and civic organizations than four-year institutions, facilitating their role in K–12 educational reform initiatives in their communities (Boswell, 2001; Orr and Bragg, 2001). As demand for college increases, community colleges are logical and appropriate institutions to link high school and college for students heretofore underrepresented in higher education.

The Academic Pathways to Access and Student Success Initiative

In 2004, with funding from the Lumina Foundation for Education, the Office of Community College Research and Leadership at the University of Illinois at Urbana-Champaign launched a new research and development initiative called Academic Pathways to Access and Student Success (APASS; www.apass.uiuc.edu). The primary goal of this initiative was to document existing and emerging academic pathways that assist high school students in fulfilling their aspirations to attend college. The APASS project examined academic pathways that have existed for some time, such as Advanced Placement, along with newer models, such as early and middle college high schools. We sought to learn how these models and approaches have been implemented and used by local educational institutions to reach diverse student populations. Our specific goals were to document the incidence of academic pathways emphasizing the high school to college transition in the fifty states, describe the underserved student groups for whom many of these pathways were created, and identify the state and federal legislation and fiscal support associated with local implementation of each pathway.

Between January 2004 and August 2005, we engaged in multiple methods of data collection, including telephone interviews with 129 state-level secondary and postsecondary officials. Between December 2004 and July 2005 site visits were conducted in seven states (Florida, Indiana, Idaho, Kentucky, Massachusetts, Oregon, and Washington), where we met with state and local officials to explore state policy and local implementation. Between December 2005 and March 2006, we followed up with e-mails and telephone calls to update information from the fifty states, and we conducted an online survey to collect information about local implementation, again with the goal of understanding how states and local entities work together to reach underserved students. Listed in alphabetical order, the APASS project documented implementation of nine academic pathways:

- Advanced Placement
- Bridge programs
- College-Level Examination Program
- Distance learning/virtual high schools and colleges
- Dual credit, dual enrollment, and concurrent enrollment
- Early and middle college high schools
- GED programs that bridge to college
- International Baccalaureate
- Tech Prep and College Tech Prep

In addition, several pathway models and initiatives emerged through interviews with state officials, including GEAR UP, career academies, High Schools That Work, charter schools, small school reforms, and high school reforms.

Results of the Fifty-State Study

This section describes the nine pathways listed, as well as national results for each pathway. Table 1.1 summarizes the overall results of the APASS project for the nine selected academic pathways; each one is described in more detail in the following paragraphs.

Advanced Placement. Created in 1955, the Advanced Placement (AP) program involves a series of courses and tests whereby high school students can earn credit at a community college, four-year college, or university by passing a standardized AP exam with a sufficiently high score. AP is administered by the College Board (http://apcentral.collegeboard.com/) and implemented by high schools in every state, making it one of the most prevalent pathways in the nation. AP has a long history as a credit-based transition program, and it can act as a vehicle to help traditionally underserved high school students make the transition to college (Bailey and Karp, 2003).

APASS results reveal that local educational organizations in forty-four states make special efforts to reach underserved students through AP programs, and of these, administrators in thirty-seven states identify AP as a way to help low-income students gain access to college. Racial and ethnic minorities and students in rural areas also receive special attention through AP in several states, and eleven (Alaska, Delaware, Florida, Georgia, Idaho, Indiana, Maine, Maryland, Massachusetts, South Carolina, Virginia) indicate that AP is a top priority to facilitate access to college. These findings are supported by a recent report from the College Board (2005) that documents progress in enrolling African American, Latino, and Native American students in AP programs over the past five years. Importantly, the proportion of Latino students among all AP exam takers in public schools now matches their overall proportion in public schools.

State-level support for the AP program is widespread. Through the APASS study, we found that a great majority of states currently or have previously provided support for AP through federal and state legislation and funding, or by establishing direct partnerships with the College Board. As well, numerous states draw on federal incentive funds to support AP programs (Martinez and Bray, 2002). Furthermore, Arizona, Colorado, Hawaii, Idaho, Montana, New Mexico, Oregon, South Dakota, and Utah, through the Western Consortium for Accelerated Learning Opportunities, are using a federal AP incentive grant to increase the number of low-income students who enroll and succeed in AP courses and exams.

Bridge Programs. Bridge programs, frequently called transition or outreach programs, are designed to provide assistance to a wide variety of youth and adult students who have difficulty accessing college. In general, bridge programs target specific student groups, including minority students, low-income students, or those with particular disciplinary interests, supporting students' academic preparation so that college-level coursework is achievable. In the APASS study, we were particularly interested in bridge programs that introduce high school juniors and seniors who demonstrate potential for attending college to the rigors of college work.

APASS results showed that bridge programs exist in forty-five states. Of those, local educational organizations in forty-two states make special efforts to assist underserved students, particularly African Americans, Latinos, and Native Americans. Although numerous bridge programs exist across the nation, data on how these programs work and how effectively they are operated are sparse. Unlike other academic pathways identified in the APASS project, state officials rarely recognize bridge programs as a priority for helping underserved students transition to college (although this is not the case in Alaska and Indiana). This is not to say that states are unsupportive of bridge programs, but rather that they operate locally, sometimes drawing on federal funds that go directly to an institution of higher education, such as funding for Upward Bound or TRIO.

College-Level Examination Program. The College-Level Examination Program (CLEP), also administered by the College Board, is a testing program that provides students with an opportunity to demonstrate college-level achievement by taking examinations that cover material taught in the first two years of the college curriculum. Many community colleges offer credit for achievements or knowledge gained outside the traditional classroom through standardized tests such as CLEP. The CLEP program was initially established by the College Board to reach out to those in the military. CLEP exams are still free for military personnel so that troops in places with little or no access to postsecondary institutions can still earn college credit. In addition, CLEP exams are promoted as a way to assist adult and working students, home-schooled students, and current college students who want to save money (College Board, 2006).

State agency respondents noted that CLEP exams are offered in community colleges and universities in forty-seven states. However, only five report making special efforts to promote CLEP in order to increase the participation

Table 1.1. Incidence and Priority of the Nine Academic Pathways

Academic Pathway	Number of States Reporting Pathway	Number of States Reporting Special Effort to Reach Underserved Students	Number of States Reporting Placing a High Priority on Pathway to Reach Underserved Students
Advanced Placement	50	45 • Low-income (37) • Racial/ethnic minority (13) • Rural (10)	11 Alaska, Delaware, Florida, Georgia, Idaho, Indiana, Maine, Maryland, Massachusetts, South Carolina, Virginia
Tech Prep/College Tech Prep	50	39 • Special populations (20) • Racial/ethnic minority (13) • Low-income (9)	10 Alaska, Delaware, Hawaii, Maine, Maryland, Massachusetts, Mississippi, Nevada, New Hampshire, Ohio
Dual credit/dual enrollment	50	29 • Low-income (11) • Racial/ethnic minority (11)	16 Arkansas, Colorado, Hawaii, Idaho, Kentucky, Montana, New Jersey, New Hampshire, North Carolina, Oregon, Pennsylvania, Texas, Utah, Virginia, West Virginia, Vermont
Distance learning/ virtual schools	50	36 • Rural (21) • Low-achieving and at-risk (8) • Low-income (6)	5 Alabama, Idaho, Massachusetts, West Virginia, Wyoming

Program				
Bridge programs	45	42 • Racial/ethnic minority (21) • Low-income (16) • Low-achieving (11)	2	Alaska, Indiana
College-Level Exam Program	47	5 • Low-achieving (2)	1	Minnesota
International Baccalaureate	49	17 • Low-income (10) • Racial/ethnic minority (5) • Rural (3)	0	
GED programs that bridge to college	43	38 • Low-achieving, at-risk, and dropout (18) • Low-income (9)	0	
Early or middle college high schools	23	21 • Low-achieving and at-risk (13) • Racial/ethnic minority (11) • Low-income (8)	3	Georgia, Massachusetts, Pennsylvania

of underserved students. Minnesota is unique among the states in its emphasis on CLEP for helping students transition from high school to college, as evidenced by the state's plan for implementing high school reform via the National Governors Association initiative (www.nga.org). Most other state officials interviewed as part of the APASS study lacked information about CLEP, and we found little capacity or interest at the state level in keeping track of students taking the CLEP exam. Nonetheless, a recent study by researchers at the College Board indicates that students who participate in CLEP programs do as well in college as students who participate in the AP program and in traditional courses (Scammacca and Dodd, 2005). External research and evaluation on CLEP's effectiveness, however, is nearly nonexistent.

Dual Credit, Dual Enrollment, and Concurrent Enrollment. Dual credit, dual enrollment, and concurrent enrollment are three related concepts. *Dual credit* means that students receive both high school and college credit for successful completion of college-level classes, whereas *dual* or *concurrent enrollment* indicates that students are enrolled in both high school and college but may not receive high school credit for their college-level courses. The term *concurrent enrollment* is sometimes applied to the dual credit earned by students who are taking a college-level course offered at their home high school.

According to the APASS study, dual credit or enrollment is one of the most prevalent academic pathways, and is present across all fifty states. Local educational organizations in twenty-nine states make special efforts to reach out to underserved student populations through dual enrollment, especially low-income, racial and ethnic minority, low-achieving, first-generation, and rural students. Forty-five states support this pathway through various policy mechanisms, and sixteen name dual credit, dual enrollment, or concurrent enrollment as a priority for increasing access to college in their state. Although policy support for this program varies among the states, thirty-eight have some type of state legislation or regulations. Similar studies by Karp, Bailey, Hughes, and Fermin (2004) and Hughes, Karp, Fermin, and Bailey (2005) on dual credit and dual enrollment policies across the fifty states show that only twelve do not have state policy that pertains to this pathway.

Two national surveys confirm the prevalence of dual credit and dual enrollment programs in American high schools and community colleges. Kleiner and Lewis (2005) found that 98 percent of public two-year institutions enrolled high school students in college courses in 2002–03. As well, community colleges are much more likely to enroll students in dual credit courses than private two-year colleges or four-year institutions. In 2002–03, 71 percent of public high schools in the United States offered dual credit courses, generating an estimated 1.2 million enrollments (Waits, Setzer, and Lewis, 2005). However, dual credit courses were more available to students attending medium or large high schools (five hundred or more enrollees), students enrolled in high schools located in towns or suburban areas, students in the central region of the country, and students attending high schools with fewer minorities. These results suggest that students' opportunities to participate in dual credit programs are not distributed equally; access depends on demographic, geographic, and economic variables.

Distance Learning and Virtual High Schools and Colleges. For the purpose of this study, the term *distance learning* is defined as instruction delivered remotely to individuals located in one or more venues (Phipps, Wellman, and Merisotis, 1998). Instruction can be delivered via various methods, including written correspondence, text, graphics, audio and video, CD-ROM, the Web, or interactive television. *Virtual schools* are synonymous with *cyberschools* at the K–12 level (Long, 2004), and *virtual colleges* refer to either secondary or postsecondary institutions that provide education through Internet-based college courses.

Results of the APASS study show that distance learning or virtual high schools and colleges exist in all fifty states and are proliferating as a means of reaching a broader base of students. Officials in thirty-six states report special efforts to reach underserved students through distance learning. Five (Alabama, Idaho, Massachusetts, West Virginia, and Wyoming) indicate that distance learning or virtual schools are a priority for increasing student access to college, and support these efforts through state allocations for online education. Many states recognize rural students—in addition to low-achieving, at-risk, and low-income students—as a target population for distance learning. In most instances, states provide financial support for distance learning through new allocations (such as in Arizona and Indiana), by redistributing general funds (such as in Missouri and North Carolina), or via a combination of both methods. Sixteen states use legislation to guide and regulate distance learning and virtual schools.

Shifting student demographics are an important factor fueling alternative educational delivery methods, and have spurred efforts to bring college-level instruction to students, rather than to expect all students to come to college. Indeed, the number of students interested in distance learning opportunities has grown dramatically in recent years (Web-Based Education Commission, 2000). As well, through partnerships between K–12 schools and community colleges (see, for example, Spears and Tatroe, 1997), several states are blending distance learning with other pathway models, such as dual credit, dual enrollment, and AP. In particular, AP, dual credit, and GED programs that bridge to college are increasingly delivered through virtual schools or the Web. Community colleges are often actively involved in developing and expanding distance learning. For example, Pennsylvania runs its distance learning project primarily through its community colleges, and Oregon offers a wide array of secondary and postsecondary distance courses to allow students of all ages to complete college degree programs.

Early and Middle College High Schools. Early and middle college high schools blend the organizational structures of high school and college through a rigorous academic curriculum (http://www.earlycollege.org). These institutions offer opportunities for students to earn a high school diploma and an associate of arts degree (or enough college credits to enter a liberal arts program at a four-year institution as a junior) within five years. Early college high schools are modeled after middle college high schools that were first developed at LaGuardia Community College (New York) in the mid-1970s. Both early and middle college high schools target at-risk or traditionally underserved students, and most are located on community college campuses.

Since their launch in 2002, early college high schools have been a fast-growing pathway model. According to a report by Jobs for the Future (2005), nineteen states had early college high schools in 2004; in 2005, early and middle college high schools were implemented in twenty-five states. Currently, seven (California, Georgia, North Carolina, Ohio, Oregon, Texas, and Utah) have statewide early college initiatives. Corroborating these results, the APASS survey found that twenty-three states had implemented this pathway model locally, and three (Georgia, Massachusetts, and Pennsylvania) indicated an intention to make this model a high priority to encourage student access to college. Special efforts to use early and middle college high schools to assist low-achieving students and racial and ethnic minorities in accessing college were reported in twenty-one states. Although support for early and middle college high schools comes mainly from foundations, in many instances it is supplemented by local K–12 funding. In California and Washington, two of the seven states with statewide early college initiatives, community colleges officially play the lead role in advancing this pathway.

General Educational Development (GED) as a Bridge to College. The General Education Development certificate, administered by the American Council on Education, is commonly referred to as an equivalent to the high school diploma. The GED was started in 1942 as a way of providing veterans who lacked a high school diploma with a chance to obtain an equivalent credential (Chaplin, 1999). It became available to nonveterans in 1952. By 1963 all fifty states administered the GED (Cameron and Heckman, 1993). For the APASS study, we were particularly interested in looking at GED and Adult Basic Education (ABE) programs that seek to link to a college curriculum and provide students with the option of completing a college degree.

Results of the APASS study show that as many as forty-three states have secondary and postsecondary educational organizations that attempt to use GED and ABE programs to help underserved students access postsecondary education. Students who are at risk of dropping out or who have dropped out, those enrolled in English as a Second Language (ESL) courses, and those who are incarcerated frequently see the GED as an entry point to college. As well, low-achieving, low-income, racial and ethnic minority, and rural students are identified as underserved student populations that local organizations in thirty-eight states are reaching through GED programs. APASS data indicate that in thirty-nine states, legislation or funding is employed to support this pathway model. GED preparatory course work is generally offered by K–12 ABE divisions, adult literacy programs, or community colleges. Community colleges play an important role in developing strategies to improve adult literacy and GED completion rates. For example, Massachusetts developed GED transition programs to help students further their education after receiving their high school equivalency.

In conjunction with K–12 ABE divisions, many community colleges offer GED programs and testing services that enhance the skills and abilities of individuals preparing for the workforce. Attempting to support implementation of these programs nationally, the National Council on Workforce Education and Jobs for the Future has launched the Breaking Through initiative, which works with sixteen community colleges across the country. On the state level, Florida's GED PLUS College Preparation Program provides GED students with the necessary skills for successful transition into college-level courses. More than 68 percent of Florida GED PLUS candidates plan to pursue higher education to expand their employment options and express aspirations to attend Florida's community colleges, technical education centers, or universities (Guglielmino, Pittman, and Vondracek, 2005).

International Baccalaureate. The International Baccalaureate (IB) diploma program, established in 1968, is intended for students in their last two years of secondary school and prepares them for college-level work. IB grew out of efforts by international schools to establish a common curriculum and a credential for entrance to universities. According to the International Baccalaureate Organization (2005), 479 IB diploma programs exist in the United States. More than twenty-five thousand American students in more than three hundred high schools participate in the IB program and constitute more than half of all IB students worldwide (Southern Regional Educational Board, 2003).

Because the IB program has existed for more than three decades, it is not surprising that this pathway model is identified by officials in forty-nine states. Yet despite a fairly large number of states that recognize IB programs, results of the APASS study show that less than half of them report special efforts to reach underserved students through IB. In addition, none of the states see this pathway as a top priority for facilitating underserved students' transition to college. In states that report making some special efforts to reach underserved students, low-income students are most frequently identified, followed by racial and ethnic minorities and rural students. Public policies related to the IB pathway are identified by officials in sixteen states. For example, Kansas and Kentucky have state policies that require all high schools to provide students with access to IB, dual credit, or AP courses. South Dakota has a state policy specifying that IB and AP credits must be accepted by public postsecondary institutions. As well, some states subsidize the IB exam fee for low-income students.

APASS data corroborate the Southern Regional Educational Board's (2003) finding that California has more schools participating in the IB program than any other state, followed by Florida. However, there is a lack of state or national research examining the effectiveness of IB programs in improving students' access to college. This may be, in part, because the IB program has been eclipsed in many states by the AP program, whose courses are accepted by most colleges and universities. Furthermore, the role of the community college in promoting the IB program appears to be very limited.

Tech Prep and College Tech Prep. Tech Prep was established in 1990 through the reauthorization of the Carl D. Perkins Vocational and Technical Education Act, and is a federally funded program promoting the integration of academic, career, and technical education. Tech Prep creates a sequential curriculum extending from high schools to community and technical colleges, and in some cases to four-year colleges and universities. Originally, Tech Prep was designed to be a combined sequence of two years of high school plus two years of postsecondary education (Parnell, 1985), but in recent years the model has been expanded to begin earlier than the eleventh grade and to extend to the baccalaureate. Some states, such as North Carolina, have adopted the label *College Tech Prep* to designate the importance of college preparation and differentiate it from secondary career and technical education (CTE). By federal law, Tech Prep programs must involve a consortium including both secondary schools and postsecondary institutions with a foundation of articulation and integration of high school and college academic and CTE coursework.

Because it is supported at the federal level, Tech Prep is recognized by all fifty states. Administrators in thirty-nine states indicate that local educational organizations make special efforts to reach underserved students; forty-nine states support the program primarily through the administration of federal funds. Since the Perkins legislation uses the particular language of "special population" as an omnibus category combining a wide range of students who are considered disadvantaged due to their racial, ethnic, economic, cultural, or physical characteristics, many states name "special populations" as the primary student group they intend to serve.

Almost all community colleges in the United States demonstrate some level of involvement in Tech Prep, and about 65 percent of consortia use community colleges as the lead institution in managing grant funds and performing administrative duties (Hershey, Silverberg, Owens, and Hulsey, 1998; Orr, 1998). Silverberg, Warner, Fong, and Goodwin (2004) estimate that 1.3 million high school students participate in Tech Prep, which accounted for 47 percent of all high schools and 10 percent of total high school enrollment in 2001. Bragg and others (2002) estimated that approximately 80 percent of Tech Prep students matriculated to college in seven of the eight consortia they studied. The percentage of Tech Prep students who continued to the community college leading the initiative ranged from a low of 16.5 percent to a high of almost 90 percent. About half of the students progressed in the same CTE program of study, suggesting that this pathway model's sequential curriculum has substantial holding power.

Conclusion

Promoting access to college is a widely accepted educational goal in the United States. However, the models and approaches available to assist students in matriculating from high school to college are wide-ranging in their intentions and outcomes. Our aim in conducting the APASS study was to provide a composite picture of academic pathways that have existed or are emerging on the national level that emphasize college access and success, including student transitions to the community college. APASS results suggest that much work lies ahead for the nine selected pathways, either individually or in concert with one another, if they are to reach underserved students in greater numbers. Many state officials are barely aware of the pathways that exist outside their borders, and some have limited knowledge of new pathways starting up inside their jurisdictions. None of the pathways that we investigated has demonstrated substantial success in facilitating students'—particularly underserved students'—transition to college. Some pathway models are receiving considerable funding from the federal government and private foundations, yet the research is far too limited to recommend particular policy mechanisms and implementation strategies for specific student groups. Even so, these developments suggest options that need to be explored if the United States is to do a better job of encouraging and supporting more of its youth to participate and succeed in college.

References

Bailey, T., and Karp, M. M. *Promoting College Access and Success: A Review of Dual Credit and Other High School/College Transition Programs.* Washington, D.C.: U.S. Department of Education, Office of Vocational and Adult Education, 2003.

Boswell, K. "State Policy and Postsecondary Enrollment Options: Creating Seamless Systems." In P. F. Robertson, B. G. Chapman, and F. Gaskin (eds.), *Systems for Offering Concurrent Enrollment at High Schools and Community Colleges.* New Directions for Community Colleges, no. 113. San Francisco: Jossey-Bass, 2001.

Bragg, D. D., Loeb, J. W., Gong, Y., Deng, C., Yoo, J., and Hill, J. *Transition from High School to College and Work for Tech Prep Participants in Eight Selected Consortia.* St. Paul: University of Minnesota, National Research Center for Career and Technical Education, 2002.

Cabrera, A. F., and La Nasa, S. M. "On the Path to College: Three Critical Tasks Facing America's Disadvantaged." *Research in Higher Education,* 2001, 42(2), 119–150.

Cameron, S. V., and Heckman, J. J. "The Nonequivalence of High School Equivalents." *Journal of Labor Economics,* 1993, 11(1), 1–47.

Chaplin, D. *GEDs for Teenagers: Are There Unintended Consequences?* Paper presented at the annual meeting of the Association for Public Policy Analysis and Management, Washington, D.C., Nov. 1999.

College Board. *Advanced Placement Report to the Nation.* Princeton, N.J.: College Board, 2005.

College Board. *Who Takes CLEP?* Princeton, N.J.: College Board, 2006. http://www.collegeboard.com/student/testing/clep/who_takes.html. Accessed Jan. 30, 2006.

Guglielmino, L. M., Pittman, S. K., and Vondracek, B. *Florida GED PLUS College Preparation Program Implementation Guide.* Tallahasee: Florida Department of Education, Division of Workforce Education, 2005.

Hershey, A. M., Silverberg, M. K., Owens, T., and Hulsey, L. K. *Focus for the Future: The Final Report of the National Tech Prep Evaluation.* Princeton, N.J.: Mathematica Policy Research, 1998.

Howe, H. *The Forgotten Half.* New York: William T. Grant Foundation, 1988.

Hughes, K., Karp, M., Fermin, B., and Bailey, T. *Pathways to College Access and Success.* Washington, D.C.: U.S. Department of Education, Office of Vocational and Adult Education, 2005.

International Baccalaureate Organization. *IB World School Statistics.* Geneva, Switzerland: International Baccalaureate Organization, 2005. http://www.ibo.org/school/statistics/progsbycountry.cfm. Accessed Jan. 27, 2006.

Jobs for the Future. *Early College Initiative by the Numbers.* Boston: Jobs for the Future, 2005. http://www.earlycolleges.org/Downloads/ECHSIByNumbersLong.pdf. Accessed May 15, 2006.

Karp, M., Bailey, T. R., Hughes, K. L., and Fermin, B. J. *State Dual Enrollment Policies: Addressing Access and Quality.* Washington, D.C.: U.S. Department of Education, Office of Adult and Vocational Education, 2004.

Kleiner, B., and Lewis, L. *Dual Enrollment of High School Students at Postsecondary Institutions: 2002–2003* (NCES Publication No. 2005–008). Washington, D.C.: U.S. Department of Education, National Center for Education Statistics, 2005.

Kurlaender, M. "Choosing Community College: Factors Affecting Latino College Choice." In C. L. Horn, S. M. Flores, and G. Orfield (eds.), *Latino Educational Opportunity.* New Directions for Community Colleges, no. 133. San Francisco: Jossey-Bass, 2006.

Lee, V. E., and Bryk, A. S. "Curriculum Tracking as Mediating the Social Organization of High School Achievement." *Sociology of Education,* 1988, *61,* 78–94.

Lee, V. E., Smith, J. B., and Croninger, R. C. "Another Look at High School Restructuring: More Evidence That It Improves Student Achievement, and More Insight into Why." *Sociology of Education,* 1995, *61*(2), 78–94.

Lewis, A. (ed.). *Shaping the Future of American Youth: Youth Policy in the 21st Century.* Washington, D.C.: American Youth Policy Forum, 2003.

Long, A. "Cyber Schools." *ECS State Notes,* Apr. 2004. http://www.ecs.org/clearinghouse/51/01/5101.htm. Accessed Aug. 19, 2005.

Martinez, M., and Bray, J. *All Over the Map: State Policies to Improve High School.* Washington D.C.: The National Alliance for the American High School, 2002.

Orr, M. T. "Integrating Secondary Schools and Community Colleges Through School-to-Work Transition and Educational Reform." *Journal of Vocational Education Research,* 1998, *23*(2), 6–25.

Orr, M. T., and Bragg, D. D. "Policy Directions for K–14 Education—Looking to the Future." In B. Townsend and S. Twombly (eds.), *Community Colleges: Policy in the Future Context.* Westport, Conn.: Ablex, 2001.

Parnell, D. *The Neglected Majority.* Washington, D.C.: Community College Press, 1985.

Phipps, R., Wellman, J., and Merisotis, J. *Assuring Quality in Distance Learning: A Preliminary Review.* Washington, D.C.: Institute for Higher Education Policy, 1998.

Rosenbaum, J. E. *Beyond College for All: Career Paths for the Forgotten Half.* New York: Russell Sage Foundation, 2001.

Scammacca, N. K., and Dodd, B. G. *An Investigation of Educational Outcomes for Students Who Earn College Credit Through the College-Level Examination Program* (College Board Research Report No. 2005–5). New York: College Board, 2005.

Silverberg, M., Warner, E., Fong, M., and Goodwin, D. *National Assessment of Vocational Education: Final Report to Congress.* Washington, D.C.: U.S. Department of Education, 2004.

Southern Regional Education Board. *Progress in Advanced Placement and International Baccalaureate in SREB States.* College Readiness Series. Atlanta: Southern Regional Education Board, 2003.

Spears, S., and Tatroe, R. L. "Seamless Education Through Distance Learning: State Policy Initiatives for Community College/K–12 Partnerships." In C. L. Dillon and R. Cintron (eds.), *Building a Working Policy for Distance Education.* New Directions for Community Colleges, no. 99. San Francisco: Jossey-Bass, 1997.

U.S. Department of Education. *Digest of Education Statistics 2003* (NCES Report No. 2005–025). Washington, D.C.: U.S. Department of Education, National Center for Education Statistics, 2004.

U.S. Department of Education. *National Postsecondary Student Aid Study 2003–04.* Washington, D.C.: U.S. Department of Education, National Center for Education Statistics, 2005.

Waits, T., Setzer, J. C., and Lewis, L. *Dual Credit and Exam-Based Courses in U.S. Public Schools: 2002–03* (NCES Report No. 2005–009). Washington, D.C.: U.S. Department of Education, National Center for Education Statistics, 2005.

Web-Based Education Commission. *The Power of the Internet for Learning: Moving From Promise to Practice.* Washington, D.C.: Web-Based Education Commission, 2000.

DEBRA D. BRAGG is professor of higher education and community college leadership, and director of the APASS initiative at the University of Illinois at Urbana-Champaign.

EUNYOUNG KIM is a doctoral student in higher education and a graduate research assistant with the APASS initiative at the University of Illinois at Urbana-Champaign.

ELISABETH A. BARNETT is senior research associate with the National Center for Restructuring Education, Schools, and Teaching at Teachers College, Columbia University, in New York, and a former APASS team member.

2

*Community colleges educate many traditionally under-
served students, including students of color, first-generation
students, and low-income students. This chapter discusses
what we know about these students, how they have fared in
college transitions, how educational pipeline and deficit
models have helped or hindered their progress, and what
community college educators should seek to understand
about this diverse population of students.*

Historically Underserved Students: What We Know, What We Still Need to Know

Denise Green

In the twenty-first century, the processes by which students move from high
school to college—including college choice, access, readiness, matriculation,
and completion—are more important than ever before. Students from all
walks of life and diverse backgrounds must negotiate these processes if they
wish to thrive in an information- and service-driven economy. However, not
all students experience these processes in the same ways; for some students,
the transition from high school to college can be extremely difficult.

For historically underserved students—defined in this chapter as low-
income students, those who are first in their families to attend college, and
students of color—gaining access to and transitioning to college can be a
great challenge. In recognition of these challenges, federal, state, and local
governing bodies have instituted policies, practices, and programs to
increase underserved populations' participation in higher education. However, two common concepts, the educational pipeline and the deficit model
(both of which will be discussed in more detail later in this chapter), miti-
gate the benefits of these programs and policies for underserved students.
Educational leaders must rethink and reframe these paradigms in order to
help historically underserved students access and succeed in college.

This chapter describes minority, first-generation, and low-income
students, many of whom attend community colleges. It focuses on what
we know about them, how they have fared in college transitions, how

NEW DIRECTIONS FOR COMMUNITY COLLEGES, no. 135, Fall 2006 © 2006 Wiley Periodicals, Inc.
Published online in Wiley InterScience (www.interscience.wiley.com) • DOI: 10.1002/cc.244

conceptualizations of the educational pipeline and deficit models have helped or hindered their progress, and what community college educators should seek to understand about this diverse population of students.

Status of Underserved Students

Most characterizations of underserved students—U.S. Department of Education studies, think tank reports, and articles from the *Chronicle of Higher Education*—tell similar stories. Many focus on the fact that graduation rates for African American, Latino, Native American, and low-income students are not at parity with the overall graduation rate (Twigg, 2005). Nonetheless, these students' aspirations to attend college remain high; over 90 percent of high school seniors plan to attend college (Venezia and others, 2005). Most underserved students attend community colleges, and these numbers are increasing as the nation experiences demographic shifts in the general population that have produced a college-going population that is more racially and ethnically diverse than ever before (Laden, 2004).

In spite of the increased numbers of underserved students attending community colleges, these students do not share the same level of success as their white and higher-income counterparts. According to Adelman (1999), the strongest predictor of college matriculation and degree attainment is a rigorous high school curriculum. However, studies consistently show that underserved students frequently do not complete a college preparatory curriculum, and often take lower-level reading and math courses (Noeth and Wimberly, 2002; Twigg, 2005). Lower achievement test scores and entrance examination scores are also common among underserved students. Not surprisingly, these characteristics do not aid the transition process from high school to college. Underserved students are more likely to delay college attendance, start their postsecondary education at a two-year institution, and attend college part-time or sporadically (Chen, 2005).

Furthermore, underserved students' "transition to college can be a time of great disequilibrium" (Rendon, 1996, p. 19). Adjusting to the academic and social demands and responsibilities of college poses many challenges for underserved students. As well, underserved students are often not as prepared as their white and higher-income peers and are more likely to need remedial courses; as a result, they are required to remain in college longer, which possibly discourages them from completing their program of study (Chen, 2005; Twigg, 2005; Venezia and others, 2005). In addition, the culture and climate of college environments that have traditionally catered to white students and those from wealthier backgrounds require minority, low-income, and first-generation students to negotiate myriad unfamiliar cultural norms, both in and outside of the classroom (Laden, 2004; Rendon, 1996; Twigg, 2005).

NEW DIRECTIONS FOR COMMUNITY COLLEGES • DOI: 10.1002/cc

Advantages and Disadvantages of the Educational Pipeline Concept

All students, including those who have been historically underserved in institutions of higher education, are expected to progress through the educational pipeline—defined as the continuous progression from high school to college and into the workforce—and ultimately become productive citizens who contribute to national, state, and local economies (Ewell, Jones, and Kelly, 2003; National Center for Public Policy and Higher Education, 2004). Conceptualizing the educational process as a pipeline is helpful to policymakers, educators, parents, and students because it illustrates both the linear and cumulative aspects of a system in which each school year or grade serves as a building block for the subsequent year or grade.

This path was once very simple, easy to anticipate, and relatively easy to plan for. Families of color and low-income families could advise their children to work hard, participate in extracurricular activities, and take advantage of programs that expose them to experiences that middle- and upper-class families routinely provide for their children, including college visits, tutoring, and preparation for entrance exams. In the 1960s, 1970s, and partially in the 1980s, a proliferation of support services, state policies, and federal programs such as Upward Bound helped underserved students recognize that college was a viable choice and ushered them into postsecondary institutions (Horn, Chen, and MPR Associates, 1998). Tutoring, summer jobs, visits to college campuses, exposure to cultural activities, and increased financial aid have all been seen as useful ways to help students move through the pipeline.

In spite of these valiant efforts, historically underserved students continue to face difficulties as they attempt to progress through the educational pipeline, and leaks at critical points of transition are leaving them vulnerable. According to a 2005 special report issued by the National Center for Public Policy and Higher Education, "the educational attainment of young Americans is declining" (p. 1A), and degree attainment for Latinos and African Americans of college-going age is less than half that of whites and Asians. The educational pipeline has become increasingly problematic for underserved students due to misalignments between K–12 and postsecondary curricula, graduation requirements, and college admissions requirements that focus heavily on high school courses taken and performance indicators, including class rank and achievement test scores. Because minority student populations are emerging as the majority in two-year colleges (Laden, 2004) and are currently the majority in many large urban school systems, they are more affected by pipeline leaks and misalignment than other students.

The educational pipeline works well when students are able to follow a prescribed sequence of courses, especially math and foreign languages, without faltering. However, underserved students consistently have problems with the lockstep sequential nature of math and language curricula and other prescribed sequences. When students falter, the alternatives are

NEW DIRECTIONS FOR COMMUNITY COLLEGES • DOI: 10.1002/cc

frequently remedial coursework, retaking courses in summer school, or leaving the college preparatory track altogether.

The more educators, parents, and policymakers understand about the structural barriers faced by underserved students, the closer the educational system will come to developing workable strategies for improving students' educational attainment. For example, the lockstep sequential nature of high school curricula needs to be made more flexible, and more curricular pathways need to be added to meet the needs of increasingly diverse student bodies. Block scheduling, online courses during the school day, pass-fail options, and a greater integration of career and academic courses could provide underserved students with alternative pathways through the pipeline.

A focus on improving states' educational or human capital—defined as the "number of highly knowledgeable, skilled people in a state's workforce"—is driving "a renewed interest in the educational pipeline concept" (National Center for Public Policy and Higher Education, 2004, p. 1). Indeed, the K–16 reform movement in a number of states has contributed to efforts to create a seamless transition from high school to college by establishing a "better alignment of academic standards, dual enrollment, and Advanced Placement" (Ewell, Jones, and Kelly, 2003, p. 1). However, each state must assess its own pipeline issues because no two states have the same combination of misalignment, student attrition, and transition problems.

In addition, educators and policymakers must pay special attention to the challenges underserved students face in persisting through the pipeline. Understandably, policymakers and educators want to help *all* students, rather than target specific populations, especially in the current environment of high accountability, limited funding, and scarce resources. Nevertheless, if we wish to halt the nation's decline in educational attainment, we must continue to ask which policies, programs, and curricula place underserved students at a greater disadvantage, and which are more successful in helping them access and succeed in college.

The Deficit Model and Underserved Students

A critical examination of the educational pipeline is needed to discern which structural elements—policies, programs, or common practices—require an overhaul. However, that examination is not possible unless administrators, policymakers, and researchers first scrutinize their over-reliance on a *deficit model*, in which minority, low-income, and first-generation college students are characterized as lacking the skills and abilities necessary to succeed in higher education. This focus on deficits emphasizes students' inabilities rather than their abilities, and encourages policies and programs that view underserved students as less than their peers who have traditionally populated colleges and universities.

The deficit model has too often biased our thinking about underserved students and provided the framework through which both K–12 and postsecondary systems have addressed transition problems (Christensen, 2004; Sautter, 1994). For many years the deficit model approach has compelled educators to focus on academic or cultural deficits that hinder underserved students' adequate adaptation to the college environment. In turn, policies, programs, and educational services have been created to cure these so-called ills.

Although approaches that attempt to fix students' deficits have shown some positive results, many underserved students continue to demonstrate negative educational outcomes. At the close of the twentieth century the nation finally began to recognize that its citizenry comprises many peoples with varying cultures and values. Furthermore, the public agrees with the sentiment that all students should be aided in reaching their greatest potential. However, the deficit model still frames many educational reforms, despite research demonstrating the negative effects of deficit thinking on underserved students (Christensen, 2004; Stanfield, 1999) and evidence of persistent, inequitable educational outcomes. Some researchers argue that the deficit model has been very harmful to students, especially those in urban school districts with a majority of low-income and minority youth (Sautter, 1994). However, hierarchical school systems, high-stakes assessment, and reactionary leadership all contribute to sustaining deficit systems (Christensen, 2004).

With respect to both math and reading curricula, the assumption based on deficit model thinking is that instruction must emphasize getting the "right answer" rather than helping students understand how answers are derived, related to each other, or could be applied in different situations (Anstrom, 1995). That is, teachers operating under a deficit model curriculum do not trust students' abilities to think critically and arrive at conclusions that approximate the right answer. The deficit model does not provide students with opportunities to think more critically, take risks, and problem-solve without penalty. Curricula that do not facilitate critical thinking restrict learning and encourage deficit thinking.

In addition to these systematic failings, underserved students encounter school personnel who emphasize their shortcomings and inability to perform in the prescribed manner. Cushman's (2005) book, *First in the Family: Advice About College from First-Generation Students*, shares students' conversations and stories, providing examples of typical encounters and how these students handled them. Situations included a teacher with low expectations, a teacher and counselor not trusting a student to do well in a particular course, and a low-income minority student fighting the low expectations of coaches. Clearly, the deficit orientation permeates student-teacher, student-counselor, and student-coach relationships and creates additional challenges and obstacles for underserved students. The deficit model encourages a self-fulfilling prophecy that nontraditional students will fail, regardless of their talents, skills, and potential (Sautter, 1994).

NEW DIRECTIONS FOR COMMUNITY COLLEGES • DOI: 10.1002/cc

What We Need to Know

To move away from this debilitating deficit orientation, researchers have advocated for a strengths-based model in which high schools and colleges "identify the positive qualities and human potential each student brings to learning. . . . The student strengths model builds learning strategies around the personal skills, interests, abilities, language, and culture of individual students" (Sautter, 1994, p. 4). If applied similarly to curriculum, leadership, and hierarchical school systems, the guiding paradigm becomes an *asset model* that incorporates positive language and labels, is visionary and strategic, and most importantly, is student-centered. Moving from a deficit to an asset model affords underserved students academic opportunities that might otherwise be unavailable to them.

Moving to an asset model requires educators to investigate the circumstances under which minority, low-income, and first-generation students succeed academically. For example, which curricular efforts facilitate academic advancement for underserved students? Which pipeline sequences help underserved students achieve academic success? Which strategies complement their strengths and career goals? Which systemic approaches minimize deficit thinking and emphasize students' strengths?

We also need to identify and share best practices from programs in which minority, low-income, and first-generation students are succeeding in college. Across the country many initiatives claim to improve all students' academic performance, but we still know very little about curriculum efforts that target specific populations. The education community understands that all students should be served, but we cannot solve problems associated with pipeline issues, deficit thinking, or limited college access without clearly confronting and understanding how current curricular pathways serve as structural barriers for underserved students.

Studies that move beyond simply collecting numerical data (such as enrollments, grades, and test scores) are needed to better understand the complex issues that affect underserved students' academic achievement. Survey, interview, and observation data provide researchers and educators with a more complete picture of the academic culture, resources, attitudes, and behaviors that promote or hinder achievement. These studies might ask if multiple curricular pathways to college foster an organizational culture, attitudes, or behaviors among teachers and administrators that help underserved students transition to college. Studies that assess how well specific pathways help minority, low-income, or first-generation students access and succeed in college would also be valuable. Furthermore, researchers might ask if there is an optimal combination of curricular pathways and support services, such as mentoring or tutoring, that can improve the likelihood of academic success.

It is also important to investigate the experiences of academically successful minority, low-income, and first-generation students. How do these students succeed despite deficit thinking and limited curricular options?

How do parents and communities aid underserved students' transition to college? These and other questions should be included in the college access and transition dialogue in order to reframe our thinking about how to best educate students who have been traditionally underserved in higher education.

Finally, we need to develop a more nuanced understanding of academic success. We all know there are different ways of being successful. However, the combination of the educational pipeline and deficit thinking forces students to either conform to a more traditional pathway or be labeled academic failures because their courses were not taken in the proper sequence or educators could not recognize their strengths. Ultimately, to truly accommodate *all* students, community college educators need to ask questions that help develop and support policies and practices that provide multiple pathways for academic success.

References

Adelman, C. *Answers in the Toolbox: Academic Intensity, Attendance Patterns, and Bachelor's Degree Attainment.* Washington, D.C.: U.S. Department of Education, Office of Educational Research and Improvement, 1999.

Anstrom, K. "New Directions for Chapter 1/Title 1." *Directions in Language and Education, National Clearinghouse for Bilingual Education,* 1995, 1(7), n.p. http://www.ncela.gwu.edu/pubs/directions/07.htm. Accessed Nov. 4, 2005.

Chen, X. *First Generation Students in Postsecondary Education: A Look at Their College Transcripts.* Washington, D.C.: U.S. Department of Education, National Center for Education Statistics, 2005. http://nces.ed.gov/pubsearch/pubsinfo.asp?pubid=2005171. Accessed Oct. 10, 2005.

Christensen, D. "Reflection of Leadership." Presentation to the Nebraska Educational Leadership Institute, Princeton, N.J., May 2004. http://www.nde.state.ne.us/COMMISH/ReflectionsonLeadership.htm. Accessed May 16, 2006.

Cushman, K. *First in the Family: Advice About College from First-Generation Students.* Providence, R.I.: Next Generation Press, 2005.

Ewell, P., Jones, D., and Kelly, P. *Conceptualizing and Researching the Educational Pipeline.* Boulder, Colo.: National Center for Higher Education Management Systems, 2003. http://www.higheredinfo.org/analyses/Pipeline%20Article.pdf. Accessed May 16, 2006.

Horn, L., Chen, X., and MPR Associates, Inc. *Toward Resiliency: At-Risk Students Who Make It to College.* Washington, D.C.: U.S. Department of Education, Office of Educational Research and Improvement, 1998. http://www.ed.gov/PDFDocs/resiliency.pdf. Accessed May 16, 2006.

Laden, B. V. "Serving Emerging Majority Students." In B. V. Laden (ed.), *Serving Minority Populations.* New Directions for Community Colleges, no. 127. San Francisco: Jossey-Bass, 2004.

National Center for Public Policy and Higher Education. "The Educational Pipeline: Big Investment, Big Returns." *Policy Alert,* Apr. 2004, pp. 1-4. http://www.highereducation.org/reports/pipeline. Accessed Nov. 4, 2005.

National Center for Public Policy and Higher Education. *State Capacity for Higher Education Policy: A Supplement to National Crosstalk.* San Jose, Calif.: National Center for Public Policy and Higher Education, 2005. http://www.highereducation.org/crosstalk/ct0305/news0305-insert.pdf. Accessed May 16, 2006.

Noeth, R., and Wimberly, G. *Creating Seamless Educational Transitions for Urban African American and Hispanic Students.* ACT Policy Report. Iowa City, Iowa: ACT, Inc., 2002.

Rendon, L. "Life on the Border." *About Campus,* 1996, *1*(5), 14–20.

Sautter, R. C. *Who Are Today's City Kids? Beyond the 'Deficit Model.'* Naperville, Ill.: North Central Regional Educational Laboratory, 1994. http://www.ncrel.org/sdrs/cityschl/c ity1_1a.htm. Accessed May 16, 2006.

Stanfield, J. "Slipping Through the Front Door: Relevant Social Scientific Evaluation in the People of Color Century." *American Journal of Evaluation,* 1999, *20*(3), 415–432.

Twigg, C. *Increasing Success for Underserved Students: Redesigning Introductory Courses.* Saratoga Springs, N.Y.: National Center for Academic Transformation, 2005. http://www.thencat.org/Monographs/IncSuccess.htm. Accessed May 16, 2006.

Venezia, A., Callan, P., Finney, J., Kirst, M., and Usdan, M. *The Governance Divide: A Report on a Four-State Study on Improving College Readiness and Success.* San Jose, Calif.: National Center for Public Policy and Higher Education, 2005. http://www. highereducation.org/reports/governance_divide/index.shtml. Accessed Oct. 10, 2005.

DENISE GREEN *is assistant professor of educational psychology in the College of Education and Human Sciences at the University of Nebraska–Lincoln.*

3

This chapter describes examples of local pathways and statewide policies that align community college standards and curricula with those at high schools and four-year colleges and universities.

Local Pathways and Statewide Policies Aligning Standards and Curricula

Andrea Conklin Bueschel, Andrea Venezia

Community colleges are often the most innovative postsecondary institutions when it comes to precollege outreach and educating underserved student populations. However, there are many roadblocks to successful reform. A lot of the work happens altruistically, person by person or campus by campus, through informal structures. There is little state policy guiding change in areas such as course placement, or in signaling academic expectations and college standards to middle and high school students. Community colleges are challenged to provide open access to all students and serve the varied needs of the community, but they must also communicate the message that there are educational standards and that students will not succeed if they are not academically prepared for college-level work. Many campuses and districts, as well as some states, are working to solve these problems in their own unique ways. This chapter highlights state and local policies and actions that attempt to streamline students' transitions between educational systems by signaling expectations more clearly and aligning standards and curricula. We focus specifically on some local initiatives as well as state-level policies in California and Florida.

Context and Challenges in Aligning Community College Standards and Curricula

Community colleges are defined by their multiple missions, diverse student bodies, and commitment to being open access institutions. Largely as a

NEW DIRECTIONS FOR COMMUNITY COLLEGES, no. 135, Fall 2006 © 2006 Wiley Periodicals, Inc.
Published online in Wiley InterScience (www.interscience.wiley.com) • DOI: 10.1002/cc.245

result of this commitment, many community college students come unprepared or underprepared for college-level work, even though almost 90 percent intend to obtain a formal credential or transfer to a four-year institution (Hoachlander, Sikora, and Horn, 2003). The community college must address each student's educational aspirations and needs and prepare him or her for further schooling or to enter the workforce.

Community colleges must also deal with the fact that there are differences in expectations at the high school and community college levels. Many students and secondary educators view community colleges as safety schools—institutions that are open to all who can benefit from their instruction. Although most community college staff support the open mission of their institutions, this characterization does not resonate with a fair number of two-year college faculty and administrators, who desire and promote high academic standards. In addition, high school teachers and postsecondary faculty often hold different views about college readiness. For example, the *Chronicle of Higher Education* recently reported that "44 percent of [college] faculty members say students are not well prepared for college-level writing, a view held by only 10 percent of [high school] teachers. . . . Thirty-two percent of faculty members say students are not well prepared in math, a judgment shared by 9 percent of teachers" (Sanoff, 2006, p. B9). If high school teachers are not clear about what it means to be college-ready, it is not surprising that students are not aware of what they will have to know and be able to do in college. The lack of clear communication across educational segments makes it difficult for community colleges to signal expectations to high school students.

Although open access is central to the community college mission, it sends confusing signals to K–12 students and other educators. Most high school students think they do not need to prepare for community college. Rosenbaum (1999) found that a sizable minority of students (46 percent) agreed with the statement, "Even if I do not work hard in high school, I can still make my future plans come true" (p. 2). These students are often surprised—usually upon receiving placement test results—by the academic standards they encounter at the community college.

Despite their institutional policy of nonselective admission, some community college programs do have selective admissions, and almost all degree-granting or transfer programs require entering students to score at a proficient level on placement exams before enrolling in college-level courses. In sum, there is a difference between gaining admission to a community college and gaining entry into its programs. Although precollegiate (or remedial) courses are offered on community college campuses, they are not considered college-level work and students do not receive transfer credit for passing them. In addition, students generally cannot fulfill degree program requirements until they have completed the required remedial courses. Focusing on access to higher education is important and necessary, but a larger challenge lies in ensuring that expectations and preparation for success are stressed just as much as access.

NEW DIRECTIONS FOR COMMUNITY COLLEGES • DOI: 10.1002/cc

Programs Signaling Community College Standards and Improving Student Readiness

Several local initiatives are working to signal academic expectations and improve students' preparation for college. This section describes California State University's Early Assessment Program as well as several other local initiatives.

California's Early Assessment Program. Community colleges in the Los Angeles Community College District are piloting the California State University (CSU) Early Assessment Program (EAP) to determine if it can help high school students improve their academic preparation for community college. EAP, a collaborative effort between CSU, the California State Board of Education, and the California Department of Education, was implemented in 2004 to provide high school students with information on readiness for college-level mathematics and English in their junior year of high school and to help them improve their knowledge and skills during their senior year. In 2005, EAP was extended to community colleges in Los Angeles; the goal of this pilot is to ensure that California high school students who enter community colleges are prepared to enroll and succeed in college-level courses. EAP is based in part on existing K–12 assessments and does not create a significant additional burden for either students or educators. If the Los Angeles pilot proves successful and enough districts are interested, it may make sense for the California Community Colleges Chancellor's Office to consider a statewide policy to widen its availability.

EAP is based on five principles. First, K–12 and postsecondary education readiness standards need to be aligned, and there should be direct assessment of college readiness standards. Second, there is a shared view of college readiness standards across institutions of higher education. Third, there should be a substantial core of K–12 standards and assessments that are aligned with college readiness standards. Postsecondary institutions should take the lead in connecting their readiness standards to K–12 standards. Fourth, the timing of assessments must be early enough to help students improve their preparation for college, and additional tests and testing time must be minimized. Finally, this work must be cost-effective (Spence, 2005).

EAP includes three components: an eleventh-grade testing program, high school preparation opportunities, and high school teacher professional development. Most of the available information is about the testing program, because it was the most challenging component to develop. The eleventh-grade assessment is based on California's Standards Tests (CSTs), the end-of-course exams all students must take. They are part of the state's testing and accountability system, are criterion-referenced, and extend to the twelfth grade (Spence, 2005).

Representatives from the CSU and K–12 systems worked together to augment the CST with mathematics and English items that measure students' college readiness in these areas. In mathematics, the items assess whether students have a deep enough knowledge of algebra and geometry. The English proficiency standards are aligned with CST standards in English-language arts, but focus more attention on students' reading and writing skills (there is a forty-five-minute essay requirement). In addition, high schools can pilot and adapt a twelfth-grade expository reading and writing course that is aligned with California's content standards. The course is geared toward preparing students for college-level English, and focuses on analytical, expository, and argumentative reading and writing.

High school students volunteer in the spring of their junior year to take the augmented CSTs. College readiness scores are calculated from a combination of performance on selected CST standard items and the augmented items. Students and their schools receive the scores in August prior to the students' senior year. Students who meet the readiness standards are exempt from additional college placement testing. Nonexempt students are guided to further instructional and diagnostic assistance in the twelfth grade, including courses and online tutorials. Students can also access the CSU Diagnostic Writing Service online or use materials from the Mathematics Diagnostic Testing Project (Spence, 2005).

California educators have learned several lessons about developing and implementing a statewide college readiness initiative such as EAP. First, state-level leadership and policy direction are needed to ensure that the same college readiness signals are given to all high schools in a state and that college readiness standards and assessments are aligned with those in the K–12 system. Educators and policymakers should continuously evaluate the match between standards, realigning if necessary. They should not rely on surrogate tests. Second, public postsecondary and K–12 education systems—especially open access institutions, because they have the potential to send the strongest, clearest signals about college readiness—must adopt the college readiness standards.

Third, colleges must emphasize placement—not admissions—policies and standards; these standards should focus on learning skills, such as reading, writing, and mathematics. Fourth, partners must define threshold performance levels and focus on a workable set of core skills. Fifth, state high school assessments should include all of the college readiness standards and a range of difficulty that is high enough to indicate whether students have mastered those standards. High-stakes tests are probably not suitable because the expected performance levels are too low and the tests might contribute to high school dropout problems. Comprehensive tests or end-of-course tests are better instruments. Finally, K–12 systems must embed college readiness standards into grades 8 through 12 curricula and assessments. This includes teacher preservice and in-service opportunities (Spence, 2005).

If the EAP effort succeeds, students entering college in California will be better prepared, will need fewer remedial classes, and will graduate in a timely fashion. In addition, the data generated will allow educators from both systems to understand students' progress through secondary and post-secondary schools and analyze the effectiveness of policy changes. However, implementing EAP throughout the California Community College system (CCC) poses some unique challenges. The CCC is under a court order to ensure that all placement exams are validated in the local context—that is, that the tests actually place students in the correct courses on that particular campus—to ensure that the tests are not biased against underserved student populations. Efforts are under way to try to add EAP tests to the list of approved placement tests that community colleges can use, which would send a signal to high school students that their course work is aligned with community college expectations and provide them with diagnostic information early enough to help them prepare for college. Thousands of community college–bound students have already opted to take the EAP to learn what they can do to improve their academic readiness for college.

Although it is still very early in the Los Angeles Community College District's pilot of EAP, their experience and findings will provide useful information for other two-year college districts in California seeking ways to make academic expectations more transparent. There is no statewide placement test in California, so each community college district adopts its own placement assessment measures, and state law requires multiple measures be used. Some of these are nationally available products developed by outside organizations (for example, ACCUPLACER from the College Board); others are locally developed tests used only by that college or district. If the EAP proves to be effective—and meets the requirements of the state—it can help to better signal expectations and provide a clearer sense of standards for college-level work.

Other Local Initiatives. Although formal programs like the EAP are not frequently implemented in community colleges, several informal partnerships have been created between a community college and its local feeder high school, or between community colleges and four-year institutions, with similar goals of signaling academic expectations for students. The assessment center at Sacramento City College, for example, offers placement tests each spring at local high schools through a program called Senior Assessment for College. High school seniors are invited to complete basic skills assessment in math and English on their high school campus, and then are invited to attend an orientation at the college. Once they complete the process (which includes some counseling) they are granted priority registration. Approximately twelve hundred students were assessed at sixteen local high schools in spring 2001.

Similarly, Maryland makes early entry and Tech Prep programs available to high school students in order to help them understand what college-level work entails. Like many other states, Maryland offers dual enrollment programs that not only provide students with a sense of what is expected in college but allow them to earn college credits while still in high school. In Oregon, Portland Community College and Mt. Hood Community College participate in a coadmissions program with Portland State University

(PSU) that helps signal to community college students what is expected at four-year institutions. Students are conditionally admitted to PSU for up to eight credit hours per term. Students who take more than eight credit hours per term must meet PSU admission requirements (Bueschel, 2004). In all of these examples, students gain a better understanding of what is expected of them and what is necessary to achieve their educational goals by participating in courses or programs at a college or university.

Local Programs Aligning Standards and Curricula

In addition to signaling expectations for overall college readiness, educators want to ensure that students' content knowledge and skills are aligned with what is expected of them in college-level classes. The Carnegie Foundation for the Advancement of Teaching has a project with eleven California community colleges that focuses on improving instruction in precollegiate English and mathematics courses. The Strengthening Pre-Collegiate Education in Community Colleges (SPECC) project works with community college faculty to examine student learning in developmental courses to find ways of reducing withdrawal rates, improving persistence to credit-level courses or the next precollegiate course in the sequence, and identifying and removing common stumbling blocks for students in English and mathematics. Although in many cases these activities focus on making learning processes visible and signaling academic expectations in a single course or a sequence of courses, the principles—and some of the activities—are applicable to a broader setting. The following paragraphs present some examples of ways that the SPECC project and its participants are working to improve students' transitions from noncredit to credit-level courses in community colleges.

The math faculty at Glendale Community College has developed a common final exam for one of its precollegiate math classes. All of the faculty members contribute questions for the exam, and it is graded based on agreed-upon rubrics. Each faculty member grades just one question for each of the several hundred exams taken each semester. The process of working together is valuable for faculty and necessary for ensuring a consistent curriculum. Students who complete and pass the course know that the whole faculty thinks they are prepared for the next level of mathematics.

The English faculty at City College of San Francisco also uses a common exam, although not as a final. Instead, the exam is offered partway through the course and provides both instructors and students with feedback about how well the material has been mastered. Again, because the students have an opportunity to learn how they are performing based on a clear standard, they will not be surprised by the level of performance expected at the next stage. By standardizing one course in the sequence, both Glendale Community College and City College of San Francisco have experienced positive changes in the courses. Although neither college has tackled the whole developmental sequence, the SPECC project and ensuing discussions have been valuable for raising awareness of the need for alignment.

In several SPECC institutions participants are exploring ways to identify common stumbling blocks to student learning. In so doing, faculty members are creating opportunities for students to think carefully about what they have learned and how it fits with their larger understanding of the topic. One activity asks students to "think aloud," or talk through what they are thinking when attempting to solve a math problem or make sense of a reading passage. Although making the student and instructor more explicitly aware of the learning process is not specifically a form of aligning standards, it is necessary in determining what the standards should be for different levels of achievement, which is the first step in alignment.

At various community colleges in the SPECC project (and in other institutions we researched), faculty members interact regularly with high school teachers, especially in the areas of math, English, and English as a Second Language. The discussions cover issues of graduation requirements, expectations, and articulation of the high school and college curriculum. Several California community colleges have worked to formalize these informal partnerships, often with outside funds. These partnerships are perfect examples of how members of different educational systems can work together to create a coherent—and ideally more seamless—transition for students.

Statewide Policies Aligning Standards and Curricula

In recent years, several states have passed legislation to better align standards and curricula between high schools and community colleges, and between community colleges and four-year institutions. This section focuses on policy in two states: California and Florida. Like many other states, California's legislation is fairly new and thus difficult to evaluate. Florida, however, has a longer history of aligning secondary and postsecondary standards, and its system applies to all students and institutions across the state.

California Policies. Recent legislation in California has focused on creating better and more aligned standards for transfer between its postsecondary institutions. Senate Bill 652 (SB 652) was adopted in 2005 and more clearly stipulates requirements for transfer between the California Community College system and the University of California (UC). There is a similar bill (SB 1785) for the community college system and California State University (CSU). Currently, there is a common course pattern for transfer from the community colleges to UC and CSU—the Intersegmental General Education Transfer Curriculum—but it identifies only some of the units a student must take for transfer; up to nine units are left to the student to choose. As the Senate Bill 652 Analysis (2005) points out, "Depending on the campus and the major the student applies to, he/she risks taking the wrong individual courses, thereby having to 'make up' courses upon arrival at UC/CSU, or potentially delaying transfer, and ultimately graduation" (n.p.).

Senate Bill 652 attempts to address this hazard. By adding a provision to the existing higher education act in California, SB 652 (2005) "requests the President of the University of California to establish a systemwide lower division transfer curriculum on or before June 1, 2006, in order to ensure a clear degree path for community college transfer students who wish to attend the University of California . . . and require the California Community Colleges, and request the University of California, to articulate, on or before January 1, 2007, the courses making up this curriculum so as to facilitate the transfer of community college students to the university" (n.p.). Although it will take time for the effects of the bill to manifest, analysis from the California Postsecondary Education Commission (2005) suggests that "the development of a more transparent and navigable path to transfer envisioned in the bill benefits both the students and the institutions" (p. 1).

Florida Policies. Of all the states, Florida has taken the most comprehensive approach to creating a statewide community college policy structure. Florida has a long history of collaboration and policy development between K–12 and postsecondary education, and community colleges in particular. Florida's community colleges play a particularly large role in educating students; over 50 percent of the upper-division students in Florida's public universities began at a community college. (For additional insights into Florida's dual enrollment policies and programs, see Chapter Four.) Florida's policies promote various strategies to achieve intersegmental collaboration.

Statewide Articulation. If students graduate from a Florida high school with a standard diploma, they are guaranteed entry into a community college. Once they earn an associate of arts degree, or an approved associate of science degree, they are guaranteed entry into a public university. In addition, the statewide articulation agreement governs many areas, including articulation between secondary and postsecondary education, admission of associate degree graduates from community colleges and state universities, the use of acceleration mechanisms, and general education requirements and statewide course numbers.

Acceleration Mechanisms. Florida offers several ways for students to accelerate their high school and college courses, such as dual enrollment, Advanced Placement (AP), and International Baccalaureate (IB). Florida colleges and universities do not collect tuition for dual enrollment courses, which eliminates competitiveness and territoriality over funds. Most of the state's dual enrollment occurs between high schools and community colleges. In 2001–02, almost thirty-three thousand high school students enrolled in ninety-eight thousand high school and community college dual enrollment courses; 80 percent passed. In addition, high schools receive more state funds for AP and IB students than they do for students in non-AP or non-IB courses.

NEW DIRECTIONS FOR COMMUNITY COLLEGES • DOI: 10.1002/cc

Common Course Numbering System. In the 1970s Florida legislators passed a bill that requires all equivalent courses at postsecondary institutions to be transferable, with few exceptions. Individual institutions control the title, amount of credit, and content of their courses, and recommend the level at which students should take the course. That information is then submitted to Florida's Department of Education, and additional standardized information (for example, the discipline, whether or not it is a survey course, and a general descriptor) is added to create a course identifier. Every course offered by a public university, community college, or vocational center must be in the common course numbering system. If a student takes a course at one institution with a course number that matches a number at another college, the latter institution has to accept that course and award the same number of credits. The common course numbering system is used in accelerated classes as well; in order for high school courses to be considered accelerated, they must use the appropriate postsecondary course number on students' transcripts. This policy allows for electronic data collection, analysis, and common transcript processes across the state. In addition, there is a single, statewide postsecondary education transcript that uses the common course numbering system. This transcript helps build and align programs between two- and four-year institutions.

Common Prerequisite Rule. The common prerequisite policy requires that every discipline in a bachelor's degree program have common prerequisites. The Florida Department of Education produces a common prerequisite manual to help community college students develop a plan to complete four-year degrees.

The Thirty-Six-Hour Rule. Florida has a thirty-six-hour policy that requires all students in postsecondary institutions to take at least thirty-six credit hours of general education to earn an associate degree. This helps to facilitate the transfer function, since all systems have the same requirement (Venezia and others, 2005, p. 14).

Conclusion

There are many challenges in creating coherent and sensible pathways for students moving between high schools and community colleges or from two- to four-year institutions. There are confusing signals, mixed messages about expectations, and misalignments of academic standards. Despite these obstacles, many educators and policymakers have sought and continue to seek ways to improve student transitions through courses, tests, and other requirements that help students achieve their academic goals. The examples offered in this chapter provide solid evidence that initiatives dedicated to improving student transitions can prosper. Although not all of the examples are scalable, they can make a difference in students' lives. With time and continued effort, these policies and practices might become the norm instead of the exception.

NEW DIRECTIONS FOR COMMUNITY COLLEGES • DOI: 10.1002/cc

References

Bueschel, A. C. "The Missing Link: The Role of Community Colleges in the Transition Between High School and College." In M. Kirst and A. Venezia (eds.), *From High School to College: Improving Outcomes for Success in Postsecondary Education.* San Francisco: Jossey-Bass, 2004.

California Postsecondary Education Commission. "Letter to California State Senator Jack Scott, April 14, 2005." Sacramento: California Postsecondary Education Commission, 2005. http://www.cpec.ca.gov/billtrack/positionletters/sb652.pdf. Accessed Apr. 11, 2006.

Hoachlander, G. A., Sikora, A., and Horn, L. *Community College Students: Goals, Academic Preparation, and Outcomes.* Washington, D.C.: U.S. Department of Education, National Center for Education Statistics, 2003. http://nces.ed.gov/pubsearch/pubsinfo.asp?pubid=2003164. Accessed May 16, 2006.

Rosenbaum, J. *Unrealistic Plans and Misdirected Efforts: Are Community Colleges Getting the Right Message to Students?* New York: Columbia University, Teachers College, Community College Resource Center, 1999.

Sanoff, A. "What Professors and Teachers Think: A Perception Gap over Students' Preparation." *Chronicle of Higher Education,* 2006, *52*(27), B9. http://chronicle.com/weekly/v52/i27/27b00901.htm. Accessed Apr. 6, 2006.

Senate Bill 652. Sacramento: California State Senate, 2005. http://www.aroundthecapitol.com/billtrack/billview.html?bill=sb_652. Accessed Apr. 11, 2006.

"Senate Bill 652 Analysis." Sacramento: California State Senate, Office of Senate Floor Analyses, 2005. http://www.aroundthecapitol.com/billtrack/analysis.html?file=sb_652_cfa_20050528_092633_sen_floor.html. Accessed Apr. 11, 2006.

Spence, D. "Early Assessment Academic Preparation Initiative." Presentation at the Wingspread Conference Center meeting hosted by the National Center for Public Policy and Higher Education, Racine, Wis., Sept. 2005.

Venezia, A., Callan, P., Finney, J., Kirst, M., and Usdan, M. *The Governance Divide: A Report on a Four-State Study of Improving College Readiness and Success.* San Jose, Calif.: National Center for Public Policy and Higher Education, 2005. http://www.highereducation.org/reports/governance_divide/index.shtml. Accessed May 16, 2006.

ANDREA CONKLIN BUESCHEL is research scholar at The Carnegie Foundation for the Advancement of Teaching, where she works on the Strengthening Precollegiate Education in Community Colleges project.

ANDREA VENEZIA is senior policy analyst and project director at the National Center for Public Policy and Higher Education.

4

This chapter presents an overview of Florida's Accelerated Mechanism Program, identifies challenges that resulted from shifting intentions behind dual enrollment policies, and shows how evolving state policy has influenced the strategies used by one college to successfully enroll underserved students and support their transition to college.

Florida's Dual Enrollment Initiative: How State Policy Influences Community Colleges' Service to Underrepresented Youth

Erika Hunt, Charles E. Carroll

In Florida, many legislators, policymakers, and parents consider dual enrollment—defined in this chapter as college courses offered to high school students for both high school and college credit—to be a very appealing educational option, because it helps address concerns about the quality of the secondary school curriculum, the costs of higher education, and the time it takes to complete a degree (Andrews, 2001; Bailey, Hughes, and Karp, 2002). As Boswell (2001) notes, policymakers are also interested in dual enrollment because it helps promote a highly trained workforce and can help prepare people to fill jobs in high-need areas such as teaching, health care, and technology. Dual enrollment is an especially attractive option for legislators who are concerned about the discontinuity of the educational continuum or who understand the need for financial or policy incentives to promote better alignment between K–12 schools and community colleges, creating pathways that allow a more seamless transition from high school to college (Michelau, 2001).

    Unlike other accelerated learning programs such as Advanced Placement (AP), which target academically gifted students, dual enrollment courses are often available to a much broader range of students—not just those who have traditionally attended college—and introduces them to college expectations, culture, and curricula (Venezia, Kirst, and Antonio,

NEW DIRECTIONS FOR COMMUNITY COLLEGES, no. 135, Fall 2006 © 2006 Wiley Periodicals, Inc.
Published online in Wiley InterScience (www.interscience.wiley.com) • DOI: 10.1002/cc.246

2003). After a brief historical overview of Florida's Accelerated Mechanism Program, this chapter identifies challenges associated with ensuring that dual enrollment courses are used to meet the needs of students, especially those of races, ethnicities, and income groups traditionally underrepresented in higher education. The chapter concludes with a discussion of the strategies one community college used to successfully enroll underserved students in its dual enrollment program.

Florida's Accelerated Mechanism Program

Florida state statute identifies three primary policy goals for dual enrollment courses: to shorten students' time to degree, to broaden the scope of curricular options available to high school students, and to increase the depth of study in a particular subject. These legislative goals reflect the circumstances that led to the creation of Florida's Accelerated Mechanism Program. Established in 1979, the Accelerated Mechanism Program is one the oldest state-sponsored academic acceleration programs in the country. The program began shortly after the release of an influential publication by the Carnegie Commission on Higher Education (1971) titled *Less Time, More Options*. Suggesting that "the length of time spent in undergraduate college education can be reduced roughly by one-fourth without sacrificing educational quality" (p. 1), the report brought national attention to the need for better integration of the secondary and postsecondary curriculum. The recommendations of the Carnegie report influenced Florida's original dual enrollment legislation, which focused on allowing students to earn a bachelor's degree in a shorter amount of time (Bickel, 1986). In the mid-1980s, the intent behind this legislation was broadened to use dual enrollment to enrich the secondary academic curriculum. As the Florida Association of District School Superintendents (2003) reports, this decision was based on the Carnegie recommendations to strengthen the high school curriculum (Bickel, 1986) as well as on the findings of the *A Nation At Risk* report.

Since then, legislators' intentions for supporting dual enrollment programs have expanded because of the special interests of different stakeholders. During the 1990s, state dual enrollment legislation focused on making dual enrollment courses available to a greater number of students and increasing student participation in the program. For example, in 1990, students attending private schools gained access to dual enrollment courses, and in 1996 legislators passed Senate Bill 186, which required home-schooled students to be included in accelerated learning programs. According to the most recent Florida Department of Education data (2002), in 2000–01, 655 home-schooled students were enrolled in dual enrollment courses at community colleges. More recent dual enrollment legislation has focused on including all eligible students. For example, House Bill 1739 (2003) amended the Florida statutes to provide access to postsecondary education for students with disabilities.

NEW DIRECTIONS FOR COMMUNITY COLLEGES • DOI: 10.1002/cc

Policymakers and educators have also paid increasing attention to the value of dual enrollment in increasing minority students' participation in higher education. The Florida Department of Education ("Governor Jeb Bush," 2004) recently published data showing the increased rates at which African American and Hispanic students who participate in dual enrollment courses later enroll in postsecondary institutions. In the 2001–02 academic year, 69.7 percent of African American high school students who took at least one dual enrollment course enrolled in college; only 44.9 percent of African American high school students who did not participate in dual enrollment classes did so. Similarly, 68.5 percent of Latino dual enrollment students enrolled in college compared to 54.3 percent of Latino high school students who did not take dual enrollment courses. In a press release issued by Governor Jeb Bush and Education Commissioner Jim Horne highlighting these data, Bush stated: "Today's numbers show that all Florida students have more opportunity. With the highest increase in dual enrollment participation among minority students, Florida continues to close the achievement gap" ("Governor Jeb Bush," 2004, n.p.). Because these dual enrollment trends align with the priorities of the federal No Child Left Behind act, dual enrollment programs are even more appealing to state decision makers.

Although Florida policy shifted in the 1990s to encourage more students to participate in dual enrollment courses, the number enrolled was still relatively small. In an effort to further increase participation in dual enrollment and other accelerated mechanisms, legislators passed a bill in 1997 that made high school and community college leaders responsible for expanding programs such as dual enrollment that allow a greater number of students to earn some college credit while still in high school. Over time, legislators enacted other policies to minimize barriers affecting the transferability of credits earned in dual enrollment courses. In 2000, the Florida legislature mandated the creation of a statewide agreement on courses and credits that meet specific high school graduation requirements (Betty Coxe, personal communication, July 20, 2001). The result was the development of a statewide common course numbering system. Under this system all credits earned in dual enrollment courses listed in the statewide directory must be accepted at all postsecondary institutions in the state. Colleges still have the ability to decide if they will count the credit as a general education credit or as an elective (Florida Board of Education, 2003).

The same legislation also required school districts to inform students of the availability of dual enrollment courses. Currently, to participate in Florida's dual enrollment program, students must be enrolled in grades 10 to 12 in an eligible school or through a home-school program. They must also submit a dual enrollment application with appropriate signatures and approvals and an official high school transcript. Students applying for associate programs must have a minimum grade point average (GPA) of 3.0 to be eligible, while students applying for certificate programs must have a 2.0 minimum GPA, meet all program entrance requirements, and be accepted by the division chairperson. Students must also provide official evidence of college-level competencies by taking the College Placement Test, ACT, or SAT, and must receive written notice of acceptance from the director of admissions at the postsecondary institution.

Policy Shifts to Address Other Educational Priorities

The intentions behind Florida's dual enrollment policies have continued to shift over the past thirty years. Today, legislators see dual enrollment principally as a mechanism to save the state money. For example, dual enrollment courses have been used to accelerate students' time to degree both in high school and in college, which has the added benefit of reducing state education costs. This intention was revealed in a study by Rasch (2004), in which interviews were conducted with twenty-four individuals, including school district and community college representatives and state policymakers. A K–12 administrator identified the financial benefits of dual enrollment in this way:

> I understand part of the goals [for dual enrollment] and . . . a lot of it actually gets back to cost. I mean when you have a state where the student population is booming, one of the ways you can save money is helping students exit or graduate from high school early. The other way you can do that is if these students can begin earning college credits before they graduate high school. Then when these students go into the community colleges or four-year universities, they will not have to be in those schools for four years. You can also save money in your Bright Future Scholarship Awards [the state's merit based scholarship program] when you only have to fund the student three instead of four years. And the other side of that is if you have students exiting from the community colleges or four-year universities early, you have more room to bring specific students from out-of-state or to serve more in-state students. [p. 136]

Thus, in addition to freeing up state funding for secondary and postsecondary education, dual enrollment courses help create space in the state's overpopulated K–12 classrooms and on college campuses. In a 2004 legislative analysis of a proposed postsecondary tuition bill, the rationale for accelerated mechanisms—including dual enrollment courses—was stated as follows: "Current law recognizes a variety of acceleration mechanisms. Acceleration mechanisms can serve as a way for students to shorten the time necessary to complete the requirements of a postsecondary degree thereby reducing the cost to the student and his or her family and providing space to increase access for additional students" (*Education Fact Sheets*, 2004, n.p.). A 2004 editorial in the *Tampa Tribune* titled "Offer Incentives, Not Penalties to Speed Up Graduation Rates" reported: "The sluggish graduation rate is a concern because Florida is experiencing explosive growth in college enrollments. The demand is taxing limited facilities and costing taxpayers, who subsidize each student to the tune of about $9,300 a year" (n.p.).

NEW DIRECTIONS FOR COMMUNITY COLLEGES • DOI: 10.1002/cc

The attempt to free up space in postsecondary institutions echoes a similar effort to alleviate the problem of overcrowded K–12 classrooms. One of the Accelerated Mechanism Task Force's assignments reported on the extent to which "secondary instruction associated with acceleration mechanism options could be offered at sites other than public K through 12 school sites to assist in meeting class size reduction needs" (Florida Board of Education, 2003, pp. 29–30).

In sum, attention to these educational priorities shifted the intentions behind dual enrollment legislation from reducing students' time to degree and expanding access to accelerated programs to using dual enrollment courses to meet other educational priorities, like addressing space and funding concerns for secondary and postsecondary education. This shift raises concerns for many who fear that legislative interest in short-term fixes, like reducing state education expenses, may overshadow policy decisions directed at meeting the long-term needs of students, particularly those from backgrounds traditionally underrepresented in higher education. According to a private school lobbyist interviewed for Rasch's (2004) study:

> I would like to make a distinction that acceleration is good public policy when students are in high school and they can access AP or dual enrollment courses because they want to access those courses and are ready to. They are at a certain level academically. That is good public policy; that is in the best interest of the individual learner. It becomes a dubious policy when we are simply just trying to fast-track kids through the system. . . . And I think you have to go back and ask yourself, what is the intent of acceleration? Is the intent to provide more courses for students who are achieving well academically so they are better prepared for college or is it more of a fiscal incentive to simply get children through high school more quickly? [p. 188]

Despite recent state policy shifts to fast-track students through high school and college, some community colleges have committed to meeting the needs of underserved students through dual enrollment courses. The remainder of this chapter focuses on one community college's strategy to successfully enroll underserved students in dual enrollment courses and support their transition to college, and discusses these strategies in the context of shifting state dual enrollment policies.

Influence of State Dual Enrollment Policy on Lake City Community College

Lake City Community College (LCCC) began as a school of forestry in 1947 and has evolved into a comprehensive, public community college serving over seven thousand students each year. The college is located in rural Florida and its district encompasses five North Central Florida counties: Baker, Columbia, Dixie, Gilchrist, and Union. This 2,683 square mile district is an area twice the size of Rhode Island. It is not uncommon for students to commute fifty to sixty miles each way to attend classes. Many students in the area are low income, and 70 percent of entering college students qualify for financial aid.

LCCC, in cooperation with the school boards of Baker, Columbia, Dixie, Gilchrist, and Union counties, as well as area private schools, provides dual enrollment opportunities for academically qualified high school students. Students attending public high schools who are enrolled in the program have tuition, book costs, and fees waived. Tuition and fees are also waived for dual enrollment students attending private high schools and those who are home-schooled.

In 2004–05, Florida passed legislation limiting class size in public schools. This legislation forced many small rural districts to increase the number of elementary school classrooms and teachers and encouraged high schools to enroll more students in dual enrollment classes. In addition, because resources were shifted away from vocational and gifted programs at the high school level, LCCC was approached by one of its school districts to take over its vocational training programs and teach vocational dual enrollment classes.

At the same time this policy took effect—essentially dismantling high school honors courses in the five counties—the number of students needing rigorous academic and vocational courses increased. This has made LCCC's dual enrollment program even more important, because it provides the only rigorous and challenging college courses available to most high school students in these five counties. The school districts' leaders, parents, and students, recognizing the importance of the dual enrollment program, supported it by more than doubling the number of students enrolled over the past three years.

Of additional concern to schools and parents was how to keep students engaged in the schooling process. In 2003–04, over one thousand students in all grade levels of the Columbia County schools were absent twenty or more days during the school year. Many high school students were not challenged by the school curricula available to them, and many dropped out. If they had been involved in academic and vocational dual enrollment programs, perhaps these students would have been encouraged to stay in school and achieve their high school diplomas.

College personnel also felt that involving students in dual enrollment had the potential to decrease the number of students requiring remediation to be eligible for college-level classes. In an area where large numbers of students were underprepared for college-level work, partially because of absenteeism in high school, any program that kept students engaged in their schooling was expected to reduce the number requiring developmental classes.

Strategies to Support Underrepresented Students in Dual Enrollment Programs. Because of the rural nature of the LCCC area and the relatively large distances between the main campus in Lake City and the outlying counties, the college developed a number of strategies to facilitate the involvement of students in dual enrollment. In addition to enrollment in on-campus courses (primarily among students from one local high school), the college hired qualified high school teachers to teach dual enrollment classes before, during, and after high school hours, sent full- and part-time college faculty to the high school locations to teach, made online classes available to students during and after school hours, connected with local schools and communities through a videoconferencing system during and after school hours, and worked with local cable television stations to provide televised classes (mainly taped) for students.

LCCC's dual enrollment courses now provide access to college courses for K–12 students in the district who might not otherwise participate in higher education. Four of the five districts offer no other acceleration mechanisms; one district offers AP courses. Over the past three years, 91 percent of students involved in LCCC's dual enrollment program averaged a C or better grade in their courses. Among the five counties, the lowest average was 89 percent and the highest was 95 percent. The overall college GPA for students in the district over the last three years was 3.2 (unweighted, out of 4.0 possible). The lowest average GPA for a student in a particular county was 3.0, and the highest was 3.4. Although longitudinal data have not yet been collected, the preliminary GPA data are promising.

Persisting Challenges. Despite the success of Florida's dual enrollment program and its obvious attractiveness to the district's students and parents, some elements continue to present challenges for LCCC and similar institutions. One area that continues to be problematic is the attitude of the state's universities toward admitting students with dual enrollment credit as opposed to AP credit. Students who transfer with an associate degree are covered under the Florida articulation agreement law, but those without the degree face problems transferring their coursework, because the universities' general attitude is that dual enrollment courses are not as academically rigorous as AP courses, in which credit is awarded via a nationally normed exam.

This is particularly troublesome when high school students apply for admission and are competing with students from other parts of the state. In awarding preference, most of the public universities give AP students one preference point but give dual enrollment students only half a preference point. Some universities do not award any preference points for dual enrollment. This is puzzling, because students who do not pass the AP test are still given preference even when they do not receive college credit for their courses. This university policy has caused a rift between the community colleges and their school districts, because high school guidance counselors try to direct students whom they believe will go immediately to a university into AP classes instead of dual enrollment programs. Furthermore, even with dual enrollment courses, the students enrolled in LCCC's four school districts that do not offer AP classes are at a decided disadvantage when applying for admission to the universities.

New Directions for Community Colleges • DOI: 10.1002/cc

Another concern is the perception among home-schooled students and their parents about their right to enroll in dual enrollment courses. Some of the parents who home-school their children are vocal about their rights under Florida law and insist on interpreting it in a way that ensures their children receive free public college education until they graduate with an associate degree. Proof of eligibility and time-to-degree requirements are spelled out clearly for public school students, but are not clearly defined in the law for home-schooled students. This issue is one to watch as LCCC continues to interpret state policies about student eligibility for dual enrollment courses.

Implications

As dual enrollment courses have garnered increasing support from legislators and state policymakers, the courses have been viewed as a mechanism through which to address a wide number of state priorities. Whether using dual enrollment courses to accelerate students through high school and college negatively influences students' educational experiences and outcomes is not yet known. The staff at LCCC and district high school counselors have expressed concern over whether students, particularly underserved students, get lost in the educational process when encouraged to progress through high school and college at a faster pace. However, there has been no evidence of this thus far. The students who seem adversely affected by dual enrollment are those who attempt to transfer credits to state universities without the associate degree, because in some instances they are not able to use their dual enrollment credits.

As the private school lobbyist interviewed by Rasch (2004) noted, legitimate motives for dual enrollment courses are those that have students' best interest in mind. Recently, Florida education policies have tended to provide quick fixes to ease the fiscal condition of the state and overcrowded schools. However, legislators in Florida and other states should be cautious about passing policies directly or indirectly related to dual enrollment. Rather than using dual enrollment as a solution to a state's fiscal problems or to relieve overcrowded classrooms, such policy decisions should be based on its ability to positively affect student learning and achievement. Only when state decision makers adopt this approach will Florida and other states be able to employ accelerated mechanisms such as dual enrollment to improve educational opportunities and success for all students.

References

Andrews, H. A. *The Dual Enrollment Phenomenon: Challenging Secondary School Students Across 50 States.* Stillwater, Okla.: New Forums Press, 2001.
Bailey, T. R., Hughes, K. L., and Karp, M. M. *What Role Can Dual Enrollment Programs Play in Easing the Transition Between High School and Postsecondary Education?* New York: Columbia University, Teachers College, Community College Research Center, 2002.

Bickel, R. "Student Acceleration: Redefining an Educational Reform." *ERS Spectrum,* 1986, *4,* 14–21.

Boswell, K. "State Policy and Postsecondary Enrollment Options: Creating Seamless Systems." In P. F. Robertson, B. G. Chapman, and F. Gaskin (eds.), *Systems for Offering Concurrent Enrollment at High Schools and Community Colleges.* New Directions for Community Colleges, no. 113. San Francisco: Jossey-Bass, 2001.

Carnegie Commission on Higher Education. *Less Time, More Options: Education Beyond the High School.* New York: McGraw-Hill, 1971.

Education Fact Sheets 2004. Tallahassee: Florida House Education K–20 Committee, 2004.

Florida Association of District School Superintendents. *A Report on Academic Acceleration Through Dual Enrollment.* Tallahassee: Florida Association of District School Superintendents, 2003.

Florida Board of Education. *Study on Accelerated Mechanisms in Florida.* Tallahassee: Florida Board of Education, 2003.

Florida Department of Education, Division of Community Colleges and Workforce Education. *In-House Report from Student Database.* Tallahassee: Florida Department of Education, 2002.

"Governor Jeb Bush and Education Commissioner Jim Horne Announce Increase in Dual Enrollment Participation Led by Minority Students." Tallahassee: Florida Department of Education, 2004.

House Bill 1739. Tallahassee: Florida House of Representatives, 2003. http://www.myfloridahouse.gov/Sections/Documents/loaddoc.aspx?FileName=_h1739er.doc&DocumentType=Bill&BillNumber=1739&Session=2003. Accessed June 28, 2006.

Michelau, D. K. *Postsecondary Enrollment Options Programs.* Denver: National Conference of State Legislatures, 2001.

National Commission on Excellence in Education. *A Nation at Risk: The Imperative for Educational Reform.* Washington, D.C.: National Commission on Excellence in Education, 1983.

"Offer Incentives, Not Penalties to Speed Up Graduation Rates." *Tampa Tribune,* May 29, 2004, n.p.

Rasch, E. L. "Dual Enrollment Within a State P-16 Education Model: A Micro-Political Perspective." Unpublished doctoral dissertation, University of Illinois at Urbana-Champaign, 2004.

Senate Bill 186. Tallahassee: Florida State Senate, 1996.

Venezia, A., Kirst, M. W., and Antonio, A. L. *Betraying the College Dream: How Disconnected K–12 and Postsecondary Education Systems Undermine Student Aspirations.* Final Policy Report from Stanford University's Bridge Project. Palo Alto, Calif.: Stanford Institute for Higher Education Research, 2003.

ERIKA HUNT works in the Center for the Study of Education Policy at Illinois State University, where she directs a statewide program aimed at strengthening the leadership of K–12 administrators in the state.

CHARLES E. CARROLL is vice president of instruction and student services at Lake City Community College in Lake City, Florida.

NEW DIRECTIONS FOR COMMUNITY COLLEGES • DOI: 10.1002/cc

Middle and early college high schools offer traditionally underserved students the opportunity to simultaneously engage in high school and college classes, with the goal of attaining both a high school diploma and an associate degree within five years. This chapter describes how two such schools support students as they confront the complexities of their educational and personal lives.

Middle and Early College High Schools—Providing Multilevel Support and Accelerated Learning

Terry Born

Adolescence is an age of border crossings. Children move from innocence to experience through experimentation, challenge, and high-stakes risk taking. They try on identities—personal, intellectual, sexual, and political—as one would change hats, always conscious that they can retreat into their childish personas if things get too dangerous. For adolescents, decisions are not forever. Relationships and commitments are not necessarily obligations. Yet as young people experiment, society simultaneously pushes back, and opportunities to grow up faster force or tempt young people to assume adult roles. The early college high school movement challenges adults and youngsters to use this period of inconstancy to build a foundation that may change the way we look at educating youth in a time of transition. If we can be successful at naming the challenges and building adequate support structures, we can channel our students' restless energy into positive accomplishments.

Middle college-early college high schools integrate high school with college in programs that graduate students with a high school diploma and an associate degree within five years. Since 2002, the Middle College National Consortium (MCNC) has served as an intermediary organization for the Bill and Melinda Gates Foundation, Ford Foundation, Kellogg Foundation, and Carnegie Corporation, all of which provide funding for the program, redesigning existing middle colleges and facilitating the opening of new early colleges throughout the country.

NEW DIRECTIONS FOR COMMUNITY COLLEGES, no. 135, Fall 2006 © 2006 Wiley Periodicals, Inc.
Published online in Wiley InterScience (www.interscience.wiley.com) • DOI: 10.1002/cc.247

49

Middle college-early colleges (referred to in this chapter as MC-ECs) offer an accelerated learning experience in a personalized, supportive environment to students who have traditionally been underserved in college. These *blended institutions* are cosponsored by community colleges and school districts and are physically located on a college campus. MC-ECs developed from the successful traditions of Middle College High School, established in 1974 at LaGuardia Community College in New York City, and foster alternatives to negative youth behaviors. They encourage close relationships between students and adults in the community and provide exposure to the college environment as a way to encourage student responsibility and commitment to academic success.

Currently, fourteen MC-ECs are in operation, and another thirteen will open within the next five years. As these institutions bridge the gap between high school and college, they face special challenges that threaten their success. MC-ECs work with students who may not be intrinsically motivated to perform academically and who generally come from homes where they are the first to graduate from high school, much less college. Many are located in communities where urban problems of violence, drug abuse, teen pregnancy, and high dropout rates are the rule rather than the exception. To overcome these obstacles, MC-ECs must carefully build a system of supports that counters some of the negative habits and influences students bring to the learning experience. Gail Mellow, President of LaGuardia Community College, named three major challenges associated with operating MC-ECs: preparing students for college-level work, helping them adjust to postsecondary education, and supporting them as they face complex personal issues (American Youth Policy Forum, 2004).

This chapter examines two MC-ECs. One of these schools has been a middle college since 1974 and is transitioning to becoming an early college. The other is a completely new early college; its first class graduated in June 2006. In this chapter, I describe and discuss the support structures that are currently employed at these two schools and the lessons that are emerging about what academic, administrative, and emotional supports need to be in place. To inform this chapter, I conducted interviews with MC-EC high school principals, faculty at the schools and their partner colleges, school counselors, and students. I consulted statistics and reports from the National Center for Restructuring Education, Schools, and Teaching, a research and development organization at Teachers College, Columbia University, and MCNC's evaluation partner. I also observed high school and college classes, as well as collaborative meetings. The following sections look at core programs that are designed to support early college students, then examine the importance of nurturing relationships at these institutions. The chapter concludes with a reflection on the way that administrative structures and communication in these two schools indirectly, but significantly, enhance or inhibit student success.

Middle College High School at LaGuardia Community College

Middle College High School (MCHS), the first middle college in the country, opened in 1974 on the campus of LaGuardia Community College. In 2002, with its sister school International High School, MCHS became the first school to reinvent itself as an early college. Currently, 193 of its 490 students are enrolled in the Excel or the early college program, which begins at the end of students' tenth-grade year. Located in an industrial area in Queens, New York, the school receives over one thousand applicants each year and accepts one hundred students who demonstrate potential for college work but have failed classes or experienced high truancy in the eighth grade. Students are ethnically diverse, and many are from single-parent homes. Most are from low-income households and receive free or reduced lunch benefits (Barnett, Kim, and Spence, 2005).

Making the Shift from a High School to a College Culture. Students interviewed indicated their motivation for enrolling in MCHS's early college program was to lessen the burden of college tuition and to accelerate and complete their college attendance early. They readily admitted that it was not an easy decision, nor was it a challenge they were prepared to meet. College instructors and their expectations alienated the youngsters, and their demands were usually nonnegotiable. Lecture formats, large classes, and scant personalization found in many traditional college classes did not coincide with the student-centered experiences with which these students were familiar. Missing class usually meant failing for a college student. Yet these students were used to missing assignments, time for revision, and second chances in high school. Early college was a shock to many students as they began to attend college classes.

Besides managing their behavior, writing is the single most important and most underdeveloped skill among students entering early college. One student who failed his first writing class remarked, "I failed it because my essays weren't strong enough. I was surprised because the instructor didn't give me enough questions or directions to build up my essays. He just destroyed me each time in class. At the end he told me I couldn't take the ACT exam in front of the class. I just cried. I felt I was attacked at the time. No teacher ever came at me directly like that. They don't have a heart."

Another student explained the difference between high school and college: "We're used to going to the teacher and the teacher tells you how you are doing. In college what they say is, 'You go to this room at this time and you get help if you want it.' They won't tell you you're failing. You could be sitting in the class the whole time, and they won't tell you [that] you are failing. The way you find out is when you get your report card." These heartfelt comments echo President Mellow's belief that college is a whole new world, with its own set of norms, its own vocabulary, and its own forms of communication. What the MCHS students were learning was that when students go to college, they either learn or they fail. At MCHS, learning about these norms and vocabulary takes place in the Early College Seminar and the summer college orientation program that occurs after students' sophomore year.

Providing Support to Students: The Role of the Seminar. MCHS's Early College Seminar is taught by high school teachers and meets two times each week during the initial summer orientation, laying the foundation for the high school to college transition. During students' junior year, the first year they enroll in college, the seminar increases to four weekly meetings of seventy minutes each. Students receive one high school credit for attendance and participation. There are currently four seminar teachers at MCHS, each of whom is expected to make contact informally with college instructors, gather college assignments, and address problems related to interschool communications or student questions and complaints. Aaron Listhaus, principal of MCHS, describes the seminar as an "informal structure, switching from whole group to individual conferencing depending on the time in the semester and what college assignments are due."

As students move forward in their college experience, this support decreases; twelfth-grade seminars meet for forty minutes four times per week. The seminar focus in this year—when students are almost entirely taking college courses—is on individual conferencing, directed to ensure fulfillment of both high school and college requirements.

Debbie Freedman, a former English teacher at MCHS who is currently a seminar instructor, describes her job as dispenser of "unlimited support." She and Randy Ohmen, another seminar instructor, share thirty-six twelfth-grade students. Freedman feels it is her obligation to be prepared to assist students with curricular issues, so she consults with college faculty, collects midterms, and reads the novels required in English classes. During the seminar, she addresses basic college requirements such as writing thesis statements and following Modern Language Association bibliographic style, but the seminar is often a time for students to catch up on their studies, type, do research, and lament about how hard it is to be a college student at age sixteen.

For students in the fifth year of the early college program (thirteenth grade), there is no formal support structure. Most have begun the separation process from MCHS and many return to the high school office only for the required daily check-in. Ann Trzcinski, early college liaison, coordinates college–high school logistics when she is not teaching high school science. She says, "I think it varies as we go from teacher to teacher and student to student. Some will still come here for support or they'll go to someone who isn't their seminar teacher . . . and say they need help. Some are just ready to fly away or don't want to admit they need help."

Debbie Freedman describes her role as responding sensitively to the "exquisite embarrassment" that students feel when they still need help during this last year. Data for students in the thirteenth grade indicate that they perform as well or slightly below their performance in the first two years of the program (Kim, Barnett, and Spence, 2006). This slight drop may be because the students take more advanced classes at this time. Nonetheless, some students graduate with honors, and others are not far behind. The average grade point averages for students in the thirteenth grade are higher than those of the general population of students at the college (LaGuardia Community College, 2006).

Currently, plans are under way to put more structure into the seminar. Instructors are hoping to formalize weekly lessons that coincide with projects and course work that will be required at the college and are adding strategies to improve students' literacy skills.

Providing Support to Students: Mentors, House, and Relationships with Caring Adults. When you speak with Debbie Freedman's students you realize the distance they are traveling or have already traveled. One seventeen-year-old senior describes his journey in this way: "You have to mold yourself into a new person. My old self wouldn't want to do a paper when the task was given. I'd [blow] it off. In college you can't do that. You have to start working as soon as it's assigned. Time is a big deal in college." Another student remarks on her discovery that one is responsible for one's own success: "You have to speak up when there is a problem." Another tells of her frustration: "For my math class [the instructor] goes so fast. In two days he would change [to a new topic], and it was too fast. Some don't help, but send you to tutoring. You have to adapt." Many students resent the changes and sacrifices they have to make to complete the degree requirements successfully and on time: "It's very hard. You don't have a lot of time, especially if you have late classes. I don't see my family 'til late at night and then I have work to do. Mostly I have a social life during vacation."

A hallmark of the MC-EC model is the relationship between caring adults and the students they instruct. The concept of *distributive counseling* is central to the middle college tradition, and MCHS has a house (advisory group), mentors, and teachers who serve as counselors. Freshman orientation groups, conflict mediation and negotiation training, and expeditionary learning through Project Adventure, an experiential learning program that builds trust, self-confidence, and focus among adolescents are ingrained in the culture of the school. Burt Rosenberg, retired principal of International High School, says, "Our students come with incredible problems. Adults attend to students' needs and every student is connected to an adult."

MC-EC students cite the critical importance of teachers who care and can be approached for assistance during rough times. Each student has a house teacher who has been a consultant, advocate, and mentor to the child since ninth grade. They meet in seventy-minute weekly group sessions to discuss academic progress, adolescent issues, and personal development. Each student also has a mentor who helps him or her with the exit portfolio and oral defense that every student must complete for graduation. They may also seek help of a more logistical nature from the early college liaison who handles all issues related to registration, testing, record keeping, and so forth. Students recognize that teachers support and appreciate them in their efforts. They are on a first-name basis with their teachers, and when there are crises in their lives, their teachers are their first resort.

Harbor Teachers Preparation Academy

Three thousand miles away from MCHS, Harbor Teachers Preparation Academy, located on the campus of Los Angeles Harbor Community College, serves approximately three hundred students in a rigorous early college program. It graduated two-thirds of its fourth-year (twelfth-grade) students with associate of arts degrees in June 2006; the remainder should complete the program during the summer or after the thirteenth grade. Three students have completed their coursework early and moved on to four-year colleges and universities. Harbor joined the MCNC in 2002 as an early college under the leadership of Principal Mattie Adams. Students are recruited from eight local middle schools and must submit to a rigorous interview and application process. Harbor's students, who are predominantly Latino and African American, are usually the first in their family to attend or graduate from college. Most meet the requirements for free or reduced-cost lunch. Like their counterparts at MCHS, they enrolled in the early college program to save tuition costs and time. (Although some Harbor students articulate the goal of becoming a teacher, most enroll in order to complete the first two years of college for free.)

Making the Shift from High School to College. Students at Harbor begin taking their college classes in the ninth grade. Looking back at his experience, one senior says students need to "be determined. Most people here are not forced. They will see that it is not fun and is hard. They can't take it for granted [that they will earn their degree]. In ninth grade it's easy, but then it gets hard." Most students intend to complete their degree requirements by their senior year in high school, a year earlier than their counterparts at MCHS. They begin the transition to college through a class called Personal Development, which is taken during their first semester at Harbor. This course, taught by a college instructor, shows students how to study, take notes, fill out study packets, and manage time—lessons that get repeated many times, from many sources, and in many venues over the next four years.

Los Angeles Harbor College eases students into college through *contract classes* for ninth and tenth graders. These courses, taught by college instructors, are attended exclusively by high school students. High school teachers accompany students, assist with behavioral issues, and sometimes intervene with support for students who are struggling. For example, in fall 2005 high school science instructors sat in on college biology classes, filling in the gaps between the high school and college curriculum. When the

NEW DIRECTIONS FOR COMMUNITY COLLEGES • DOI: 10.1002/cc

course appeared difficult for many students, high school teachers developed study packets that helped students pass the course. At Harbor, the mantra is "Study! Study! Study!" and assistance usually means students need to do more: show more self-discipline, read material again, attend afterschool tutoring or Assignment Workshop, a homework help session. The consistent repetition that students are responsible for their own success has its rewards—students recognize their ability to control their future. As one senior said, "You have to understand that being here isn't a walk through the park. You actually have to work."

Students are also immediately immersed in the sometimes-unpleasant realities of college. Due to space and budgetary constraints, contract classes are generally crowded, lecture-driven, and may last for as long as three hours. Ninth-grade students at Harbor are registered for physical education, health, and music or art. Tenth graders take either an ancient civilizations class or biology, as well as a foreign language and child development. Eleventh graders enroll independently in required and elective courses after meeting with high school or college counselors. The number of eleventh and twelfth graders permitted to enroll in the same college class is limited to five, which decreases options for study groups, common projects, or griping about the coursework.

The few students whose grade point average falls below 3.0 are permitted to register for only one college course. The philosophy is that by the time students are in the eleventh grade, they will have had the foundations and habits of mind ingrained in their first two years at the school and be ready for the unfiltered college experience. Classes at the high school are geared toward helping students pass California's High School Exit Exam and CAT-6 examinations, and AP courses are also offered in social studies.

Providing Support to Students: Advancement Via Individual Determination (AVID). The basic way in which student support is provided at Harbor is through the Advancement Via Individual Determination (AVID) program. AVID teachers, who include most of the staff, receive training in the philosophy and skills of the program. Leadership for AVID rests with one teacher-leader, who organizes activities, disseminates information, and meets regularly with the staff. The class meets four days per week and offers instruction, tutoring, and personal support. Students are taught Cornell note-taking and time-management skills and are coached in how to study. They are given advice and practice in timed writing assignments, prewriting, and research skills.

In tutorial sessions, all students are required to bring in a question or problem from their academic classes, and they are coached in how to write appropriate questions. Teachers check the questions at the door as students enter. If they arrive at AVID without a tutorial question they are penalized. Questions are divided into three levels: simple yes and no, questions of analysis, and questions that depend on prediction. If the teacher sees there is a classwide question, the class works as a unit. If the students need to discuss

NEW DIRECTIONS FOR COMMUNITY COLLEGES • DOI: 10.1002/cc

different questions, they work in small groups. Solutions are derived from peers, either by sharing the answer or by working the problem out together. These rituals develop students' understanding that questions are a road map to solutions, build peer support for academic improvement, and often lead to clarification and understanding of the hard concepts they grapple with in their high school and college classes. Although the AVID program is structured, it adapts when the need requires.

Providing Support to Students: Other Strategies. The counseling structure at Harbor is oriented toward educational concerns. Advisory sessions are bimonthly, and students participate in values clarification exercises and discuss good habits. A high school counselor performs programming, credit checking, and record-keeping duties. A college counselor, available part-time, assists with preparations to move students into four-year institutions upon graduation. Students move about the campus freely, talk informally—but respectfully—to the staff, and enjoy a confidence that comes with knowing they are truly cared for, safe, and well liked. One student says, "The teachers have surprised me. I will never be this close to my teachers again. You can talk to them or hang out in their classrooms at lunch. I think the one who helped me the most was Dr. O. He talks to you. He's taught me that it's not about the teacher. It's about yourself. You have to convince yourself you can be in a college class. You can do the work. If you can't control your emotions, you can't be in a college class."

As the school has grown, Harbor faculty and administrators have seen changes in the student body. The first cohort saw themselves as pioneers. They were on a mission. Students who entered after the first group are sometimes not as committed or as fiercely determined to meet the rigorous demands. Teachers meet regularly to brainstorm and design appropriate strategies for these youngsters. Teachers, teaching assistants, and interns from a neighboring four-year college also offer a scheduled tutoring program. Some students reach out to peers for assistance. Students who fall behind in homework are required to attend homework help sessions. AVID teachers keep records and students serve detention for failure to attend.

Reflections on the Approaches of Two Schools

Academic and personal guidance supports are the obvious pillars that hold up students in MC-EC programs. When we define the enterprise of MC-EC as a border crossing, it is not only the students who have to make that passage. High schools and colleges entering into this venture also take steps to bridge the gaps between the institutions and build structures that make their new identities and expectations transparent to students. Students expect that courses will be hard and college instructors less forgiving, nurturing, or patient than their high school teachers. What they do not understand are the written and unwritten rules of the college process. Prerequisites, credits, appointments, and the question of withdrawal versus failure in a college class are not in teenagers' vocabularies, and many students are vocal in their indignation about the lack of information they receive.

Students at both schools expressed frustration at being shut out of courses or made to wait long periods of time between high school and college classes. They were anxious about the possibility of not being able to graduate on time if all their high school and college requirements were not complete. Some had never seen their transcripts or recently learned that they were short one or two courses required to earn a degree. This problem arises in part from the developing structure of the early college model. Each state has its own high school graduation requirements. High schools and colleges must carefully review which college courses are legally permitted to replace the high school courses. They must examine their curricula to ascertain if these courses prepare students for state exams. Five-year graduation plans that meet both high school and college requirements need to be firmly established, clearly explained, and available to all constituents.

Although they are different, both MCHS' and Harbor Teachers Preparation Academy's approaches to student support work well. They provide stable, consistent adults who bolster students' self-esteem and serve as positive and mature role models. These teachers and counselors provide academic support and are advocates for students who may not have experienced the luxury of an adult's trust and willingness to go out on a limb for them. Yet each school has a small population of students who do not succeed in the cultural limitations and freedoms inherent in either the middle college or early college models. At both MCHS and Harbor, the most highly at-risk students either fade out and withdraw or draw negative attention to themselves through inappropriate behaviors.

Students at schools such as Harbor, which approach all student communications through the lens of academic performance, are successful for several reasons. Such schools send students the message that school is important, their futures are important, and therefore, *they* are important. However, for teens in crisis there is great comfort and strength to be derived from schools such as MCHS, where they can take the time and find a safe haven to let go, stop, cry, scream, or just say "Help!" The larger community of MC-EC high schools needs to discuss both of these approaches and explore some middle-ground solutions that will allow them to provide the ideal combination of academic and personal support.

References

American Youth Policy Forum. *Small High Schools and Early/Middle College High School: An American Youth Policy Forum Field Trip—January 8–9, 2004.* Washington, D.C.: American Youth Policy Forum, 2004. http://www.aypf.org/tripreports/2004/tr010804.htm. Accessed Jan. 25, 2006.

Barnett, E., Kim, J., and Spence, K. *Early College Student Survey Report: Academic Year 2004–05.* New York: Columbia University, Teachers College, National Center for Restructuring Education, Schools, and Teaching, 2005.

NEW DIRECTIONS FOR COMMUNITY COLLEGES • DOI: 10.1002/cc

Kim, J., Barnett, E., and Spence, K. "Middle College–Early College Participation and Course Enrollments, 2004–05." Unpublished raw data. New York: Columbia University, Teachers College, National Center for Restructuring Education, Schools, and Teaching, 2006.
LaGuardia Community College. *Institutional Profile*. Long Island City, N.Y.: LaGuardia Community College, 2006. http://www.lagcc.cuny.edu/facts/. Accessed Jan. 25, 2006.

TERRY BORN *is former principal of Robert F. Wagner Jr. Secondary School for Arts and Technology and currently serves as a coach for the Middle College National Consortium.*

NEW DIRECTIONS FOR COMMUNITY COLLEGES • DOI: 10.1002/cc

6

This chapter examines community college baccalaureate programs and the controversy surrounding these programs. It also looks at models for the delivery of these baccalaureates, emphasizing their curricular focus in states and colleges across the nation. The chapter concludes with questions that should guide decision makers in enhancing student access and bachelor's degree completion.

Achieving the Baccalaureate Through the Community College

Deborah L. Floyd

Community and junior colleges have a rich history of providing access to the baccalaureate degree through various means and models while limiting their own highest award to the associate degree. Two-year colleges are usually easily accessible to community members and thus are conveniently positioned to serve as a focal point for educational partnerships. And as they have evolved from junior colleges to comprehensive institutions, contemporary community colleges have demonstrated their commitment to baccalaureate partnerships through various models. These include *articulation models,* whereby students are guaranteed that their credits will transfer to a four-year institution; *university extension models,* in which universities provide extension programs leading to the baccalaureate degree; *university center models,* including a variety of on-site partnerships designed to help students earn a baccalaureate (conferred by universities); and finally, *community college baccalaureate models,* whereby the community colleges themselves (not universities) confer the degree (Floyd, 2005). Although most community college presidents indicate a preference for partnership models, as opposed to delivering and conferring baccalaureates independently (Community College Baccalaureate Association, 2003; Floyd, 2005), there is an undeniable trend across the United States and Canada for two-year institutions to make a bid to offer their own baccalaureate degrees in specialized curricular areas.

This chapter describes models of community college baccalaureate (CCB) delivery in the United States, focusing on community colleges that

NEW DIRECTIONS FOR COMMUNITY COLLEGES, no. 135, Fall 2006 © 2006 Wiley Periodicals, Inc.
Published online in Wiley InterScience (www.interscience.wiley.com) • DOI: 10.1002/cc.248

have obtained authorization to do so in certain curricular and degree areas. The chapter also explores the myths and realities of the somewhat controversial CCB degree and offers strategies for implementing CCB programs.

This chapter is based on analysis of college and university Web sites, newspaper and periodical articles, proposed and current state legislation, working papers and policy documents, discussions with community college practitioners, and unpublished presentations by practitioners and scholars at the 2003, 2004, 2005, and 2006 Community College Baccalaureate Association conferences. It also relies on previously published and edited work (Floyd, 2005; Floyd, Skolnik, and Walker, 2005; Floyd and Walker, 2003) referencing models, state approvals, and general information about colleges.

Myths and Realities of the Community College Baccalaureate

Contrary to the belief of some, the CCB is not a recent phenomenon. New York's Fashion Institute of Technology gained approval to grant fashion degrees in the 1970s, and West Virginia's Parkersburg Community College obtained approval to grant baccalaureates in the 1980s. What is new, however, is the momentum with which community colleges are gaining approval, and the consistent curricular emphasis on meeting local employment and workforce demands.

The notion of community colleges conferring their own baccalaureate degrees is wrought with controversy and passionate arguments on both sides (Eaton, 2005; Mills, 2003; Townsend, 2005; Walker, 2001). Many critics fear that CCB degrees shift the colleges' focus away from their core community mission and bread-and-butter curricular offerings—developmental, transfer, community, and technical education—toward inappropriate priorities, such as upper-division baccalaureate courses that lead to four-year degrees. But advocates of the CCB degree see this as a myth rather than the reality, and assert that the new CCBs respond to expanding workforce needs that are not being met by universities.

Although some believe that universities should confer all baccalaureate degrees, as universities increase undergraduate admissions standards and place more emphasis on research and graduate studies they deemphasize certain university degrees, including those offered for place-bound students and those in disciplines such as teacher education, technology, middle management, and allied health. Thus, advocates for the CCB argue that community colleges are justified in seeking authority to offer these degrees, especially if there is a strong community need. To advocate for the CCB, the Community College Baccalaureate Association (CCBA) was formed in 1999. The CCBA includes members from twenty-eight states, four Canadian provinces, Bermuda, Jamaica, research institutions, private industry, and higher education institutions (Walker, 2005).

A common myth, especially among decision makers with limited understanding of this new trend, is that CCBs are traditional liberal arts degrees that are more appropriately offered by universities. In reality, these degrees are overwhelmingly applied workforce degrees in such areas as technology, management, business, nursing, law enforcement, agriculture, engineering, and teacher education.

Another myth about community colleges is that they are and have always been two-year colleges that do not offer post-baccalaureate courses and programs. In reality, community colleges have delivered post-associate degree training for years through their continuing education programs in areas such as teacher certification, allied health, legal studies, and fire science. In fact, students in noncredit continuing education classes (again, mainly in workforce-related areas) account for about half of the ten million students enrolled in United States community colleges each year (American Association of Community Colleges, 2000). Proponents of the CCB see workforce and applied baccalaureates as necessary and valid credentials to prepare students for the workforce, a core community college mission.

Nevertheless, traditionalists such as Eaton (2005) and Wattenbarger (2000) hold steadfast to the belief that universities should continue to be the gatekeepers of baccalaureate degrees; they encourage community colleges to partner with four-year institutions to create university centers and greater articulation. In some cases, however, these university–community college partnerships do not result in students receiving desired curricular programming locally; this is especially difficult for place-bound students (Floyd, 2005). Without the CCB, these students would likely be denied access to baccalaureate degrees.

Another myth is that the CCB will cause community colleges to try to become full-fledged four-year institutions. It is true that in the last ten years or so, a handful of junior and community colleges have evolved into four-year state colleges or have become university branches or two-year extensions of universities that grant baccalaureate degrees. However, these numbers are extremely low compared to the historical number of public and private junior or community colleges that have evolved into four-year institutions for reasons other than the CCB. This myth is largely unfounded, and states with swelling populations and limited or no four-year state colleges— such as Florida, Arizona, and Nevada—may be justified in looking to community colleges to fill the state public college void, especially in high-demand professional fields such as teacher education.

Yet another common myth is that community colleges need to strengthen partnerships to address local demands for baccalaureate degrees. In reality, most community colleges with baccalaureate degree approval already have strong partnerships with four-year colleges and universities— the new CCB degrees are often added as a curricular complement. Community colleges have been programmatically addressing issues of access to the baccalaureate for many years through partnerships such as university centers and concurrent-use programs (Windham, Perkins, and Rogers, 2001), and presidents actually prefer partnership models when practical (Floyd, 2005). Most of the time, the new CCBs are offered in high-need technical disciplines for which a local university has no specialized faculty or that the institution simply chooses not to offer.

Baccalaureate Delivery Models in Community Colleges

It is not a simple task to count and identify community colleges conferring their own baccalaureates, because current systems of classifying community colleges are imperfect. For example, the name of the community college offering these degrees may not always include the word "community." Until recently, the Southern Association of Colleges and Schools (SACS), which accredits community colleges in large states such as Florida and Texas, required that community colleges approved to offer at least one baccalaureate degree drop "community" from their name and become classified as four-year colleges. By early 2006, the SACS Commission on Colleges had softened its position, and Florida's Daytona Beach Community College and Florida Community College at Jacksonville won the right to keep "community" in their college names. Furthermore, colleges such as the University of Arkansas at Fort Smith and the University of West Virginia at Parkersburg (formerly Westark Community College and Parkersburg Community College, respectively)—both of which are affiliated with universities—are included in some but not all tallies of CCB institutions because they are no longer community colleges by title. Because of these classification problems and little published research, it is difficult to determine precisely which institutions offer the new baccalaureates and how the programs are delivered.

And there are other puzzles to solve. Should baccalaureate degrees conferred by community colleges that were later classified as four-year colleges still be considered CCBs? Should baccalaureate degrees awarded by an institution affiliated with a university, but formerly approved only for associate degrees, be considered a CCB? If an institution considers itself to be a community college, but awards baccalaureate degrees (and some master's degrees) in a field such as fashion design, is that institution offering the CCB? The Community College Baccalaureate Associate organization says yes to all of these questions, and in 2003 it began embracing institutions that offer baccalaureates through one or more of the partnerships described in the sections that follow (K. P. Walker, personal communication, January 13, 2006). Regardless of the term used to describe these institutions, many associate degree–granting institutions are seeking authorization to offer and confer specialized baccalaureate degrees and are incorporating diverse and creative models to do so (Skolnik and Floyd, 2005).

Articulation Model. Most community colleges have agreements with universities to ensure their acceptance of freshman and sophomore credits, and some of these agreements are more formal than others. States such as Texas, Illinois, New York, California, Oklahoma, Tennessee, and Washington have transfer rates above the national average because their community colleges and universities formally collaborate to ensure that their students' credits transfer (Wellman, 2002). Creative partnerships such as those of Florida's Brevard Community College (BCC) and the University of Central Florida (UCF) not only guarantee admission to community college graduates but give them preferential status for admission to selective programs. The BCC and UCF partnership includes bold plans to increase shared faculty and double the number of degrees at regional campuses to increase baccalaureate access (Dean, 2006). Although this articulation model is effective in providing access to the baccalaureate, it is not always practical for place-bound students who cannot relocate or for students who are unable to articulate entry to specific programs of study.

University Centers and Concurrent-Use Campus Models. University centers and concurrent-use campuses are becoming increasingly popular ways of providing access to the baccalaureate because they allow community colleges to partner with one or more senior colleges and universities to deliver baccalaureates degrees locally. Lorenzo (2005) lists six models for university center and concurrent-use campuses: the *colocation model,* in which institutions share the same space; the *enterprise model,* where institutions form a consortium to operate a higher education center; the *integrated model,* in which a higher education center is integrated on a community college campus; the *virtual model,* which is similar to campus-based university centers, but in which upper-level course work is offered online; the *sponsorship model,* where the community college is in charge of operating the university center and determining curricular offerings; and the *hybrid model,* in which community colleges confer some baccalaureate degrees but also partner with universities for other degrees, including graduate degrees. With the exception of the hybrid model, all of these arrangements designate the senior college or university to confer the degree, not the community college.

Another creative partnership is the *embedded baccalaureate model,* a concept describing the partnership between Northwestern Michigan College, Macomb Community College, and Ferris State University (Cotto, Teahen, and Thomas, 2006). This model emphasizes learning outcomes, curricular alignment, transparency for students, shared responsibilities for advising and leading student programs, and seamless transitions between terms and courses. Students participating in this unique model graduate with both associate and baccalaureate degrees.

University Extension Model. Community colleges such as Hawaii's Maui Community College, Arkansas' Westark Community College, and West Virginia's Parkersburg Community College are affiliated with universities and have merged their governance structures, although some are more aligned than others. In other states, such as Louisiana and Oklahoma, land-grant state universities have been awarded authorization to operate associate degree branches that are not community colleges per se, but function much like them in serving local needs.

To illustrate, in 2003 and 2004, respectively, Louisiana State University-Alexandria and Oklahoma State University-Okmulgee were approved to offer select baccalaureate degrees; previously, their highest offering was the associate degree (Floyd, 2005). Although these colleges have "university" in their names rather than "community," the challenges they face in gaining degree approval for baccalaureate programs are quite similar to those faced by community colleges. As Table 6.1 illustrates, six states (Arkansas, Georgia, Louisiana, Utah, West Virginia, and Oklahoma) recently authorized associate degree institutions to offer baccalaureates. Some of these institutions are a part of land-grant universities, others have converted to state colleges.

Community College Baccalaureate Model. This chapter defines a "pure" CCB as one coming from public community colleges or two-year institutions that are approved to confer baccalaureate degrees in one or more areas. This category does not include partnership models wherein the colleges themselves do not confer baccalaureate degrees, although associate-only colleges approved to add baccalaureates are often included in these counts, as noted earlier. Nine states have approved these baccalaureates: Florida, Hawaii, Indiana, Nevada, New Mexico, New York, Texas, Vermont, and Washington.

Florida has led the United States in the development of contemporary CCBs. In 2001, Florida's oldest community college, St. Petersburg College, was the first in the state approved to offer its own baccalaureate degrees. The authorizing legislation specifically addressed the need for workforce programs in high-need areas such as information technology, nursing, and teacher education. Subsequently, legislation was passed authorizing other community colleges to offer specific baccalaureate programs as long as they were developed to meet identified workforce needs and could not be offered through an existing partnership with a university.

As Table 6.2 illustrates, seven Florida community colleges were authorized to offer baccalaureate degrees in 2006. These CCBs are designed to meet workforce needs in teacher education, business and management, health and allied health, and agriculture. Almost all of Florida's CCBs are bachelor of applied science or bachelor of applied technology degrees, which are applied workforce designations. However, bachelor of science degrees are awarded in various teacher education disciplines.

Table 6.3 notes the curricular areas of focus for CCBs in Vermont, Texas, New Mexico, and Washington. Texas authorized three community colleges to offer bachelor of applied technology degrees to meet specific local workforce needs. Although Vermont Technical College offers a bachelor of arts in general education, most of its CCBs are bachelor of science degrees in technology, management, business, engineering, and architectural disciplines. New Mexico recently authorized New Mexico Community

Table 6.1. Recent Examples of Baccalaureate Authorizations, by State

State	College	New Name	Degrees Offered/Curricular Focus	Time Line
Arkansas	Westark Community College	University of Arkansas-Ft. Smith	BAS; added BS, BA, and BME later: Manufacturing technology	In 1997 authorized up to nine baccalaureate degrees; became a four-year college in 2002.
Georgia	Dalton Junior College	Dalton State College	BS, BAS, BSW: Management studies, industrial operations, information systems, technology, social work, early childhood education	Became a four-year college in 1998 after offering "focused" baccalaureates in management and workforce fields.
	Macon Junior College	Macon State College	BS and BSN: Communications and information technology, health information, public service, business, health services, nursing	Became a four-year college in 1996; focuses on "concentrated market-driven" degrees in allied health, business, and services.
Louisiana	Louisiana State University-Alexandria	No change	BGS, BS, BLS: Elementary education, general education, biology, liberal studies	Legislation in 2001 authorized offering baccalaureate degrees.
Oklahoma	Oklahoma State University-Okmulgee	No change	BT: Information assurance and forensics, instrumentation engineering technology, civil engineering technology	Approved by Oklahoma State University Board of Regents in 2004.
Utah	Utah Technical College	Utah Valley State College	BAT, BA, BS; also BFA in various other disciplines: Community health, information technology	Became a four-year college in 1993.
	Dixie College	Dixie State College	BS: Business administration, computer information technology, elementary education, nursing	Became a four-year college in 2000.
West Virginia	Parkersburg Community College	University of West Virginia at Parkersburg	BAT, BA, BS, RBA (Regents BA): Business administration, elementary education, applied technology, business	In 1989 became affiliated with the University of West Virginia; in 1993 gained legislative authority to offer baccalaureate.

NEW DIRECTIONS FOR COMMUNITY COLLEGES • DOI: 10.1002/cc

Table 6.2. Community College Baccalaureate Programs in Florida

College Name, April 2006	Education	Technology, Management, and Business	Law Enforcement and Service	Health and Allied Health	Agriculture and Engineering	Year Initially Approved
Daytona Beach Community College		BAS: Supervision and management				2005
Florida Community College at Jacksonville			BAT: Fire technology			2005
Edison College			BAS: Public safety management			2005
Okaloosa-Walton College		BAS: Project and acquisitions management				2003
Chipola College	BS: Secondary education, secondary biology education					2002
Miami Dade College	BS: Exceptional student education, secondary math, secondary science					2002
St. Petersburg College	BS: Elementary education, exceptional student education, secondary math, secondary education	BAS: Technology, management; BAS: Technology, education	BAS: Public safety, administration	BAS: Dental hygiene, orthotics, and prosthetics; BS: Nursing	BAS: Veterinary technology	2001

NEW DIRECTIONS FOR COMMUNITY COLLEGES • DOI: 10.1002/cc

Table 6.3. Community College Baccalaureate Programs in Vermont, Texas, New Mexico, and Washington

College	Education	Technology, Management, and Business	Law Enforcement	Health and Allied Health	Agriculture and Engineering	Year Initially Approved
Vermont Technical College	BA: General education	BS: Business technology and management, computer engineering technology, information technology, software technology			BS: Architectural engineering technology, electromechanical engineering technology	1993 (six degree programs approved since then)
Midland College (Texas)		BAT: Technology, management				2003
Brazosport College (Texas)		BAT: Technology, management				2003
South Texas College		BAT: Technology, management				2003
New Mexico Community College	BA: Elementary, secondary, early childhood, special, and bilingual education					2004
Washington State Board for Community and Technical Colleges	In 2005, the Washington legislature authorized a pilot program allowing four community colleges to offer baccalaureate degrees starting in 2007. The Washington State Board for Community and Technical Colleges selected four colleges in April 2006: Bellevue Community and Technical College (BAS in radiation and imagining sciences); Peninsula College (BAS in applied management); Olympic College (BSN in nursing); and South Seattle Community College (BAS in hospitality management). Programs selected should serve workforce needs primarily for place-bound students. Degrees will be applied baccalaureates. Up to three other community colleges may be selected for fiscal support through partnership university contracts wherein the university awards the baccalaureate.				2005 and 2006

College to offer bachelor of arts degrees in the high-need fields of elementary education, early childhood education, special education, and bilingual education. In 2005, Washington State's legislature authorized a pilot program to allow four community colleges to offer baccalaureate degrees to meet identified workforce demands for place-bound students. The Washington State legislation also authorized three pilot university partnerships in another effort to increase the state's baccalaureate attainment. In 2006, four community colleges, Bellevue Community and Technical College, Peninsula College, Olympic College, and South Seattle College were selected for the new CCB degrees (Borofsky and Seppanen, 2006). The colleges are located in suburban, rural, and urban areas, as well as in a Navy town, and will focus on delivering specific applied science degrees to meet specific workforce demands.

Nevada and Hawaii's community colleges are governed by the same state boards that govern the universities. In 1999 Nevada's Great Basin College, which serves the rural area surrounding Elko, was authorized to confer workforce bachelor of arts and bachelor of science degrees in teacher education, business, technology, and professional studies. Great Basin College added a bachelor of science degree in nursing in 2005. In 2004 the Community College of Southern Nevada was approved for a bachelor of science degree in dental hygiene, again to address local employment needs. Maui Community College was approved for workforce baccalaureates in applied business and information technology in 2003.

Issues, Challenges, and Strategies in Implementing CCB Programs

Illinois, Arizona, California, Michigan, and South Carolina all have seen recent legislative activity or are conducting studies or authorizing state-level task forces to look at community colleges and baccalaureate degree delivery. Perhaps this bubbling activity is due, in part, to a lack of university responsiveness to place-bound students or specific academic majors. It may also be the result of increased consumer demand for relevant locally delivered baccalaureates, especially in technical and workforce fields. According to Ignash and Kotun (2005), states are responding to consumer demand for technical and occupational baccalaureates, and associate degrees are no longer considered terminal awards. In response to such demand, thirty-one states have career ladder pathways leading to technical and professional associate degrees. Because bachelor's degrees are required for entry to a greater number of career fields, educational leaders and policymakers are looking to creative models for fitting technical and occupational courses into the baccalaureate degree framework. Based on recent trends, local, state, and federal leaders will continue to be challenged well into the future to discover how best to deliver relevant training and education to meet identified workforce and consumer needs.

NEW DIRECTIONS FOR COMMUNITY COLLEGES • DOI: 10.1002/cc

When considering enhancing baccalaureate completion through community colleges, decision makers would be wise to research needs for specific degrees before deciding which delivery system or model is most appropriate. Community colleges are quite experienced in expeditiously conducting needs assessments and program reviews, and in developing relevant course and program offerings to meet identified community and workforce needs. The questions and processes for planning and implementing relevant certificate and associate degree programs are almost identical to those involved in creating bachelor's degree programs, although the politics are quite different. Before selecting a specific delivery model, leaders should ask questions and be open to creative answers.

Assessment, Goal Setting, and Planning Phases. During the assessment, goal setting, and planning phases, educational leaders should ask the following questions: What are the needs of the local workforce and who will be served? Why is a particular bachelor's degree needed? Will stakeholders, such as employers, support these new degree programs? Is the community college president willing to champion these efforts? Are these programs congruent with the mission of community colleges? Who are the target students, and what evidence exists that these students need and want the program? What are the political ramifications of this program, both in and outside the college? What are the political ramifications of selecting one model over the other? What authorizations are required for each model from accreditors, legislators, or local and state boards? Is there adequate funding to implement the program, and will the funds be recurring and sustained or limited to the short term? Who will work to ensure the new programs are successful? Are resources such as libraries, facilities, staffing, student services, reporting, and equipment necessary? Which models offer the most appropriate delivery systems for baccalaureate degrees?

Leaders should take the time to conduct realistic assessments, set goals, and make plans. This phase has the potential to energize stakeholders and partners in high schools, communities, businesses, universities, and political arenas as systems and cultures are challenged. Community colleges should use this time to let their creative juices flow, freshen their missions, engage partners, listen to student and employer needs and wants, and empower organizations and people. They should take this opportunity to visit campuses that implement similar programs, and include stakeholders such as faculty, staff, student affairs personnel, and community leaders in meaningful ways early in the planning processes. Stakeholder buy-in is critical in maneuvering the challenges of change and the various layers of necessary approvals.

Approval, Implementation, and Monitoring Phases. Change takes time. Anecdotal stories from community college presidents who led their colleges through the challenges of gaining approval to confer their own baccalaureates often talk about how much longer the process took than they expected. Politics should not be underemphasized, because last-minute political maneuvers may derail authorization. This occurred in 2004, when

Trident Technical College (TTC) in South Carolina made plans to offer its own bachelor's degree in culinary arts. Although the legislature overrode the governor's veto of the program, TTC's plans were derailed at the state board and commission levels. Local, state, and national politics greatly affect the process of finding the best model for specific baccalaureate programs. Persistence and patience have been beneficial in several states where community colleges have had to make multiple bids for baccalaureate degree authority before finally gaining approval. Frequently, the most cumbersome aspect of this phase is gaining approval from the accrediting association—a step that is often required even if the community college does not confer the degree, because most accrediting associations require approval of substantive programmatic changes, such as university center partnerships.

Once an approach or model has been selected and approved for delivery, and assessments, goals, and plans have been developed, the next steps are implementation and monitoring, which are not simple. Successful new programs should not fall by the wayside if a key CCB advocate, such as the president, leaves. To ensure sustainability, systems and teams should be developed at various levels so stakeholders buy in to the new program and devote time to ensure its goals are achieved. Surprises can be minimized with the use of appropriate implementation and monitoring systems and through collaborative teamwork.

Evaluation Phase. The evaluation phase is important as a formative and summative effort. Throughout the processes of change, leaders should ask if they are accomplishing their goals and if their actions are congruent with the missions of the institution. Are the students successful and if so, in what ways? If not, why? What are the indicators of success, and what were the program's outcomes on these measures? How can evaluation be used to improve the program? Over time, is the program still necessary or should it be dissolved if workforce needs are met? What are the program's effects on the college's climate? Finally, the most obvious and important question is this: Is the college doing this for the right reason—its students? If the answer is an honest and ethical *yes*, then community college leaders have a solid foundation on which to build new CCB programs. If, however, these programs are being developed for reasons such as politics, status, and ego, they have no place at a community college.

Concluding Thoughts

The United States is not alone in addressing the challenges of educating a competitive workforce by increasing access to the baccalaureate and creating new baccalaureate degrees (Laden, 2005; Levin, 2004; Skolnik, 2005). Although this chapter does not address applied baccalaureates in Canada, it is important to note that a growing number of community colleges in several Canadian provinces are implementing applied baccalaureate degrees (ABDs). Laden (2005) and Skolnik (2005) note that Canadian ABDs are offered in some but not all provinces, and are concentrated in specialized technical curricular areas that lead to employment and respond to local economic needs. Walker and Floyd (2005) define the ABD in the United States as an applied workforce baccalaureate degree that, on completion, allows graduates to "apply what they are learning to real-world situations" (p. 96). They also note differences between traditional baccalaureates and the new applied workforce baccalaureates. In particular, ABDs are developed in collaboration with employers and use applied and contextual learning methods, as opposed to traditional academic pedagogy. Although no formal classification system exists to define clearly community college ABDs and applied workforce baccalaureates, according to the research done for this chapter, these skill-based baccalaureates often result in degrees such as bachelor of technology, bachelor of applied science, and in certain technical fields, bachelor of science.

Community and junior colleges in the United States and elsewhere have created and forged new academic pathways to the baccalaureate by articulating degrees and classes, through partnerships with university centers, and by offering stand-alone workforce baccalaureate degrees. Throughout history, institutions of higher education have continuously evolved. Such changes are stimulated by emerging community needs, by students' desires for convenience and relevance, and by shifting priorities inside colleges and universities. Change in the past has been more evolutionary than revolutionary, and that continues to be the case. Achieving the baccalaureate through the community college is an appropriate and increasingly popular pathway for large numbers of students in the twenty-first century.

References

American Association of Community Colleges. *National Profile of Community Colleges: Trends and Statistics* (3rd ed). Washington, D.C.: Community College Press, 2000.

Borofsky, D., and Seppanen, L. "Washington State Principles, Criteria and Process for Selecting CTC Applied Bachelor's and University Contract Pilots." Paper presented at the annual International Conference of the Community College Baccalaureate Association, Atlanta, Mar. 2006.

Community College Baccalaureate Association. *Baccalaureate Needs Assessment Survey. Unpublished Survey Results.* Ft. Myers, Fla.: Edison College, Community College Baccalaureate Association, 2003.

Cotto, M., Teahen, R., and Thomas N. "Embedded Baccalaureates—New Concepts, Enduring Relationships." Paper presented at the annual International Conference of the Community College Baccalaureate Association, Atlanta, Apr. 2006.

Dean, J. "BCC Graduates Guaranteed UCF Admission." *Florida Today,* Apr. 5, 2006. http://www.floridatoday.com.

Eaton, J. S. "Why Community Colleges Shouldn't Offer Baccalaureates." *Chronicle of Higher Education,* 2005, 52(10), B25. http://chronicle.com/weekly/v52/i10/10b02501.htm. Accessed May 22, 2006.

Floyd, D. L. "Community College Baccalaureate in the U.S.: Models, Programs, and Issues." In D. L. Floyd, M. L. Skolnik, and K. P. Walker (eds.), *Community College Baccalaureate: Emerging Trends and Policy Issues.* Sterling, Va.: Stylus, 2005.

Floyd, D. L., Skolnik, M. L., and Walker, D. A. (eds.). *Community College Baccalaureate: Emerging Trends and Policy Issues.* Sterling, Va.: Stylus, 2005.

Floyd, D. L., and Walker, D. A. "Community College Teacher Education: A Typology, Challenging Issues, and State Views." *Community College Journal of Research and Practice,* 2003, 27(8), 643–663.

Ignash, J. M., and Kotun, D. "Results of a National Study of Transfer in Occupational/Technical Degrees: Policies and Practices." *Journal of Applied Research in the Community College,* 2005, 12(2), 109–120.

Laden, B. V. "The New ABD's: Applied Baccalaureate Degrees in Ontario." In D. L. Floyd, M. L. Skolnik, and K. P. Walker (eds.), *Community College Baccalaureate: Emerging Trends and Policy Issues.* Sterling, Va.: Stylus, 2005.

Levin, J. S. "The Community College as a Baccalaureate-Granting Institution." *Review of Higher Education,* 2004, 28(1), 1–22.

Lorenzo, A. L. "The University Center: A Collaborative Approach to Baccalaureate Degrees." In D. L. Floyd, M. L. Skolnik, and K. P. Walker (eds.), *Community College Baccalaureate: Emerging Trends and Policy Issues.* Sterling, Va.: Stylus, 2005.

Mills, K. "Community College Baccalaureates: Some Critics Decry the Trends as 'Mission Creep.'" *National CrossTalk,* 2003, 11(1), n.p. http://www.highereducation.org/crosstalk/ct0103/news0103-community.shtml. Accessed May 22, 2006.

Skolnik, M. L. "The Community College Baccalaureate in Canada: Addressing Accessibility and Workforce Needs." In D. L. Floyd, M. L. Skolnik, and K. P. Walker (eds.), *Community College Baccalaureate: Emerging Trends and Policy Issues.* Sterling, Va.: Stylus, 2005.

Skolnik, M. L., and Floyd, D. L. "The Community College Baccalaureate: Toward an Agenda for Policy and Research." In D. L. Floyd, M. L. Skolnik, and K. P. Walker (eds.), *Community College Baccalaureate: Emerging Trends and Policy Issues.* Sterling, Va.: Stylus, 2005.

Townsend, B. K. "A Cautionary View." In D. L. Floyd, M. L. Skolnik, and K. P. Walker (eds.), *Community College Baccalaureate: Emerging Trends and Policy Issues.* Sterling, Va.: Stylus, 2005.

Walker, K. P. "Opening the Door to the Baccalaureate Degree." *Community College Review,* 2001, 29(2), 18–28.

Walker, K. P. "History, Rationale, and the Community College Baccalaureate Association." In D. L. Floyd, M. L. Skolnik, and K. P. Walker (eds.), *Community College Baccalaureate: Emerging Trends and Policy Issues.* Sterling, Va.: Stylus, 2005.

Walker, K. P., and Floyd, D. L. "Applied and Workforce Baccalaureates." In D. L. Floyd, M. L. Skolnik, and K. P. Walker (eds.), *Community College Baccalaureate: Emerging Trends and Policy Issues.* Sterling, Va.: Stylus, 2005.

Wattenbarger, J. "Colleges Should Stick to What They Do Best." *Community College Week.* 2000, 13(18), 4–5.

Wellman, J. V. *State Policy and Community College-Baccalaureate Transfer.* San Jose, Calif.: National Center of Public Policy and Higher Education and the Institute for Higher Education Policy, 2002. http://www.highereducation.org/reports/transfer/transfer.shtml. Accessed May 22, 2006.

Windham, P., Perkins, G., and Rogers, J. "Concurrent Use: Part of the New Definition of Access." *Community College Review,* 2001, 29(3), 39–55.

DEBORAH L. FLOYD *is professor of higher education leadership and program leader at Florida Atlantic University in Boca Raton. She has over twenty-five years of administrative experience in community colleges as a president, vice president, and dean.*

NEW DIRECTIONS FOR COMMUNITY COLLEGES • DOI: 10.1002/cc

7

*This chapter examines recent attempts to promote
students' transitions into postsecondary education. In
particular, it focuses on the evolution of career and
technical education (CTE) to promote student transition
by coupling more rigorous academic preparation with
CTE programs.*

The Role of Career and Technical Education in Facilitating Student Transitions to Postsecondary Education

Donna E. Dare

A recent report to the Lumina Foundation (Bragg and Kim, 2005) created a broad context for addressing student transition from high school to college by defining academic pathways as "boundary spanning curriculum and organizational structures that bridge K–12 with higher education to facilitate student transition to college" (p. 1). Vocational education, or career and technical education (CTE), is one academic pathway that is continuing to emerge as a boundary-spanning approach to facilitating students' transition from high school to postsecondary education. Once considered a *track* for non-college-bound high school students, CTE has evolved to include an increased emphasis on rigorous academic preparation and integrated and articulated CTE courses and programs. According to the Association for Career and Technical Education (2006), CTE is now a "major enterprise within the United States' P–16 education system" (p. 9).

In the past, CTE has been viewed as an undesirable curricular track, one suitable only for students who will not go to college. Today, many high schools offer CTE that requires advanced academic skills to help students make the transition to college-level technical and professional studies. Indeed, DeLuca, Plank, and Estacion (2006) and Hudson and Hurst (1999) found that participation in a blended CTE and college preparatory curriculum prepares students for both college and work. In an examination of

cohorts of students in four high schools between 1982 and 1994, Hudson and Hurst found that mathematics and reading achievement test gains between the eighth and twelfth grades for those who participated in a combined college preparatory and vocational program were not statistically different from those for students who completed only a college preparatory curriculum.

Specifically, of a group of students scoring in the middle two quartiles on eighth-grade math assessments, students who completed a concentration of secondary CTE courses along with a college preparatory curriculum increased their mathematics test scores by an average of twenty-seven points by the twelfth grade; students from the same two quartiles who completed only a college preparatory curriculum gained an average of twenty-nine points. By comparison, students from the same two quartiles who only took a CTE concentration gained twenty-two points. Reading test score gains for the same group of students were twenty-one points for the combined curriculum, twenty-two for the college prep curriculum, and eighteen for the CTE concentration. In addition, 1992 public high school graduates who completed a combined CTE concentration and college preparatory curriculum were about as likely to enroll in postsecondary education as those who completed only a college preparatory curriculum (90 and 94 percent, respectively). By comparison, students who completed only a CTE concentration, and those who enrolled in a general curriculum, were much less likely to enroll in college (52 and 70 percent, respectively). Although the number of students in Hudson and Hurst's (1999) study who took courses that spanned the CTE and academic boundaries was small, it increased markedly between 1982 and 1994, from 0.6 percent in 1982 to 4.5 percent in 1994. Further, the U.S. Department of Education (2004) recently reported that secondary students participating in CTE increased their enrollment in academic courses over the past decade and demonstrated higher academic achievement than previous cohorts. Although only about 13 percent of all high school graduates participated in combined CTE and academic programs, these results offer strong evidence that those who do are as well prepared as students who only took a college preparatory curriculum—and far better prepared than students who took a CTE concentration but who did not complete a rigorous academic curriculum—to successfully transition to college.

Participants in the 2003 National High School Leadership Summit (U.S. Department of Education, 2003) noted that the once-common assumption that CTE does not prepare students for higher education is no longer valid. Newer models include helping CTE students meet high academic and technical expectations, easing CTE students' transitions to postsecondary education and advanced training, and increasing the rigor of CTE instruction. Summit leaders cited several models of comprehensive high school reform that combine academic preparation with CTE to support students in attaining education beyond high school.

This chapter describes four best-practice programs that combine CTE courses with rigorous academic curricula. Two of these programs, High

Schools That Work (HSTW) and Tech Prep, focus on infusing rigorous academic lessons into CTE to prepare students to enter and succeed in college. Both of these initiatives have demonstrated at least moderate success in improving students' academic achievement and have played a significant role in advancing education reform (Bottoms, Feagin, and Han, 2005; Bragg, Reger, Brown, Orr, and Dare, 2002). The second two programs, the College and Career Transitions Initiative (CCTI) and Project Lead the Way (PLTW), span academic disciplines to develop vocational students' academic skills and invite relevance and application into the traditional academic classroom. These two initiatives build on key curricular strategies (namely, integration and articulation) used in HSTW and Tech Prep, combining academic and CTE to prepare students to meet the demands of college and careers (Bottoms and Young, 2005; Hoachlander, 2006; U.S. Department of Education, 2003).

Patterns that lead to successful enrollment in and completion of college cannot and will not change unless the pathways that lead to postsecondary education also change. That change requires, in part, creative approaches that bridge the gaps between K–12 and community college systems and recognize the key role community colleges play in the education continuum.

High Schools That Work (HSTW)

Since 1987, high schools offering HSTW have implemented reforms aimed at preparing all students, including traditionally non-college-bound students, for further learning and employment. This initiative has focused on ten key practices, including high expectations, rigorous CTE and academic studies, work-based learning, teachers who work together, actively engaged students, guidance, and a culture of continuous improvement (Southern Regional Education Board, 2005). In over one thousand high schools in thirty-two states, HSTW reforms have emphasized replacing general high school curricula with rigorous academic courses paired with CTE classes. Their goals are increased academic achievement and college readiness for 85 percent of all students, as well as increased performance on National Association of Education Progress–referenced reading, mathematics, and science tests.

Students participating in the nine HSTW studied by Bottoms and Anthony (2005b) showed gains in academic achievement, largely because strategic goals for supporting academic preparedness for college became standard operating procedure. These nine schools eliminated lower-level academic courses and raised graduation requirements to exceed state requirements. Five of the schools adopted a career pathways model and required students to select a broad career path by ninth or tenth grade. All classes included writing- and reading-intensive coursework. All schools emphasized literacy and academic preparation for all students, and each offered CTE dual credit courses through its local community colleges.

Bottoms and Young's (2005) study of HSTW revealed patterns in student transitions. For example, 90 percent of students who completed the

HSTW-recommended academic core enrolled in postsecondary studies, compared to 75 percent of noncompleters. Furthermore, only 24 percent of students who completed the recommended academic core were required to take remedial courses, compared to 34 percent of students who did not complete the core. In addition, high school graduates who completed a sequence of at least three CTE courses in a broad career field were just as likely to enroll in postsecondary institutions as other graduates. Thus, although their strategies for reform are leveraged primarily at the high school level, HSTW can also affect postsecondary outcomes.

Tech Prep

Since its inception in the early 1990s, Tech Prep has focused on integrating academics with CTE courses and on partnerships between secondary and postsecondary education that support students' transition to college. Tech Prep has accomplished these goals through articulating courses and programs, curriculum development, professional development, collaboration with business and industry, work-based learning, and career and educational planning. Although the National Association of Vocational Education (U.S. Department of Education, 2004) argued that Tech Prep is not a comprehensive reform model, and pointed out significant problems associated with identifying and tracking outcomes for Tech Prep students due to inconsistent implementation, Bragg, Reger, Brown, Orr, and Dare (2002) indicated that several exemplary sites across the country were successfully transitioning students to college, particularly in schools in which the Tech Prep initiative evolved into a College Tech Prep model. College Tech Prep emphasizes academic rigor along with CTE course-taking, as well as innovative approaches to articulation and dual credit. Like HSTW, Tech Prep served as a catalyst for the expansion of dual credit and dual enrollment programs across the country and helped educators sequence and align courses and programs across institutional boundaries (Bragg, Reger, Brown, Orr, and Dare, 2002).

College and Career Transitions Initiative (CCTI)

Although many reforms over the past two decades have focused on strategies for changing high schools, CCTI emphasizes community colleges' responsibility to play a greater leadership role in partnering with high schools to facilitate the transition of students into postsecondary education and employment, and to improve students' academic performance at both the secondary and postsecondary levels (Hughes and Karp, 2006). CCTI's goals include facilitating students' transitions from high school to college and careers, increasing student success, building partnerships with high schools and businesses, reducing the amount of remediation required by incoming students, learning about and developing career pathways, and offering dual or concurrent enrollment opportunities (College and Career Transitions Initiative, 2005).

CCTI's goal is to create pathways from secondary to postsecondary education. According to Hughes and Karp (2006), the strength of the program lies in the implementation of policies that support alignment between K–12 and postsecondary systems. For example, CCTI staff convene state policy forums to advance career pathway programs that have demonstrated promise in supporting students' academic preparation and transition to college.

Project Lead the Way (PLTW)

Organized around specific career clusters, PLTW breaks down curricular barriers, provides rigorous and relevant instruction, and promotes students' preparation for further education. Currently implemented in over one thousand high schools across the country (Hoachlander, 2006), PLTW's rigorous academic design couples college prep academic courses and challenging CTE studies to promote students' transition into engineering careers (Bottoms and Anthony, 2005a). Building on theories of constructivism and the benefits of applied academics and contextual teaching and learning, PLTW introduces students to a gamut of careers involving engineering and engineering technology through five sequenced courses. Students learn relevant knowledge and skills in math, science, and engineering through projects and learning activities that are based on real-world problems. PLTW is also developing curricula for other career cluster areas.

Although PLTW was first developed in the 1980s, outcomes for students who have participated in PLTW are limited to date; most research has focused on PLTW implementation rather than outcomes. In a report on its first-year implementation of outcomes assessment, TrueOutcomes (2005) questioned the PLTW approach but lauded its potential to positively influence student transitions: "Despite the fact that the objectives were not met, PLTW students attend college and pursue engineering and engineering technology at much higher rates than the national average, which is very positive" (p. 27). PLTW's popularity and rapid expansion is due at least in part to the very high goals it has set. Specifically, 90 percent of PLTW graduates are expected to successfully complete a first year of postsecondary education and 75 percent are expected to finish a two- or four-year program in engineering or engineering technology. Although these goals have not yet been realized (only 68 percent of graduates thus far have indicated their intention to pursue engineering or engineering technology degrees in college), longitudinal findings should be available in three to six years.

Nonetheless, Bottoms and Anthony (2005a) indicate that, when compared to similar students from other CTE fields, PLTW students show significantly higher performance in reading, math, and science on National

Association of Educational Progress–referenced assessments. They also complete significantly higher-level math and science courses, enroll in programs that emphasize reading and writing across the curriculum, demonstrate skill in solving real-world problems by using technology and working in groups, and use academic knowledge and skills to complete project assignments. A slightly higher percentage of PLTW students (72 percent) than students from comparable CTE fields (69 percent) indicate intent to enroll in postsecondary education.

Conclusion and Recommendations

Initiatives like HSTW, Tech Prep, CCTI, and PLTW serve as wake-up calls for community colleges. Initiatives that target high school students who do not fit the traditional college student profile bring significant challenges for community colleges. One key strategy for addressing these challenges is to move beyond specific elements of individual programs to identify common, crosscutting situations that require consistent and effective leadership, management, and integration.

For example, articulation and course sequencing exist in some form in all the CTE initiatives outlined in this chapter. Rather than dealing with each program discretely or randomly, community colleges should provide leadership in developing articulation-related policies and practices that support all students in their transition to college. Similarly, all CTE initiatives emphasize career and educational planning. Although high school CTE programs vary, community colleges must provide key leadership throughout students' transition processes.

As learning and workforce needs evolve, and as key initiatives like HSTW, Tech Prep, CCTI, and PLTW provide more data to document their successes, educators are pushing historically discrete educational boundaries. Community colleges now have a range of models to use in partnering with high schools and supporting students' transitions to postsecondary education. Community colleges need to provide leadership in supporting transition efforts.

Today's learners are less bound to space, place, and time than any prior generation of learners. Colleges and universities must learn to meet students' needs and demands while they are still in high school and help them transition into college and the workforce. Community colleges, in particular, are well positioned to partner with high schools to offer learning opportunities to students through articulated credit, dual credit, and dual enrollment programming.

In addition, programs and initiatives that blend CTE with rigorous academic coursework are providing students with increasingly advanced sets of precollege learning experiences. Community colleges must be ready to meet these students' needs and help them attain their educational and career goals.

References

Association for Career and Technical Education. *Reinventing the American High School for the 21st Century: Strengthening a New Vision for the American High School Through the Experiences and Resources of Career and Technical Education.* Alexandria, Va.: Association for Career and Technical Education, 2006. http://www.acteonline.org/policy/legislative_issues/upload/ACTEHSReform_Full.pdf. Accessed May 25, 2006.

Bottoms, G., and Anthony, K. *Project Lead the Way: A Pre-Engineering Curriculum That Works. A New Design for High School Career/Technical Studies.* Atlanta: Southern Regional Education Board, May 2005a. http://www.sreb.org/programs/hstw/publications/briefs/05V08_Research_PLTW.pdf. Accessed Dec. 28, 2005.

Bottoms, G., and Anthony, K. *Raising Achievement and Improving Graduation Rates: How Nine High Schools That Work Sites Are Doing It.* Atlanta: Southern Regional Education Board, 2005b. http://www.sreb.org/programs/hstw/publications/briefs/05V14_Research Brief_raising_graduation_rates.pdf. Accessed Dec. 28, 2005.

Bottoms, J. E., Feagin, C. H., and Han, L. *Making High Schools and Middle Grades Schools Work. U.S. Department of Education, Institute of Education Sciences Final Report, October 1999–March 2005.* Atlanta: Southern Regional Education Board, 2005. http://www.sreb.org/programs/hstw/publications/special/05V12W_Making_HS_MG_Schools_Work.pdf. Accessed Dec. 28, 2005.

Bottoms, G., and Young, M. *High Schools That Work Follow-Up Study of 2002 High School Graduates: Implications for Improving Transitions From High School to College and Careers.* Atlanta: Southern Regional Education Board, 2005. http://www.sreb.org/programs/hstw/publications/briefs/05V10_Research_Follow-up_2002_Graduates.pdf. Accessed Dec. 28, 2005.

Bragg, D. D., and Kim, E. *Academic Pathways to Access and Student Success: A Lumina Foundation Grantee Report.* Champaign: University of Illinois at Urbana-Champaign, Office of Community College Research and Leadership, 2005. http://www.apass.uiuc.edu/publications/lumina_grantee_report.pdf. Accessed Jan. 12, 2006.

Bragg, D. D., Reger, W., Brown, C. H., Orr, M. T., and Dare, D. *New Lessons About Tech Prep Implementation: Changes in Eight Selected Consortia Since Reauthorization of the Federal Tech Prep Legislation in 1998.* St. Paul: University of Minnesota, National Research Center for Career and Technical Education, 2002.

College and Career Transitions Initiative. *A Career Pathway.* Phoenix: League for Innovation in the Community College, 2005. http://www.league.org/league/projects/ccti. Accessed Mar. 1, 2006.

DeLuca, S., Plank, S., and Estacion, A. *Does Career and Technical Education Affect College Enrollment?* St. Paul: University of Minnesota, National Research Center for Career and Technical Education, 2006. http://www.nccte.org/publications/infosynthesis/r&dreport/DoesCTEAffectCollegeEnrollment/DoesCTEAffectCollegeEnrollment.html. Accessed Mar. 1, 2006.

Hoachlander, G. "Ready for College and Career." *The School Administrator,* Jan. 2006, n.p. http://www.aasa.org/publications/saarticledetail.cfm?ItemNumber=4917&snItemNumber=950&tnItemNumber=951. Accessed May 23, 2006.

Hudson, L., and Hurst, D. "Students Who Prepare for College and a Vocation." *National Center for Education Statistics Issue Brief,* 1999, *1*(4), 1–2.

Hughes, K. L., and Karp, M. M. *Strengthening Transitions by Encouraging Career Pathways: A Look at State Policies and Practices.* Washington, D.C.: American Association of Community Colleges, 2006. http://www.aacc.nche.edu/Content/ContentGroups/Headline_News/February_2006/9287_AACCvisualreport.pdf. Accessed Feb. 27, 2006.

Southern Regional Education Board. *High Schools That Work: An Enhanced Design to Get All Students to Standards.* Atlanta: Southern Regional Education Board, 2005. http://www.sreb.org/programs/hstw/publications/2005Pubs/05V07_enhanced_design.pdf. Accessed May 15, 2006.

TrueOutcomes. *Report on the First Year of Implementation of the TrueOutcomes Assessment System for Project Lead the Way.* Clifton Park, N.Y.: TrueOutcomes, 2005. http://www.pltw.org/TrueOutcomesReport_05v4.pdf. Accessed May 25, 2006.

U.S. Department of Education. *Charting a New Course for Career and Technical Education.* High School Leadership Summit Issue Paper. Washington, D.C.: U.S. Department of Education, Office of Vocational and Adult Education, 2003. http://www.ed.gov/about/offices/list/ovae/pi/hsinit/papers/cte.pdf. Accessed Nov. 5, 2005.

U.S. Department of Education. *National Assessment of Vocational Education: Final Report to Congress.* Washington, D.C.: U.S. Department of Education, Office of the Under Secretary, Policy and Program Studies Service, 2004. http://www.ed.gov/rschstat/eval/sectech/nave/navefinal.pdf. Accessed Jan. 12, 2006.

DONNA E. DARE *is director of Career and Technical Education at St. Louis Community College, Missouri.*

The Miami Valley Tech Prep Consortium, headquartered at Sinclair Community College in Dayton, Ohio, engages a wide range of students in Tech Prep pathways that span high school and college. Students are offered a blend of technical and academic coursework, as well as extensive supports enhanced by a sophisticated professional development system. The outcomes include low rates of remediation and high rates of graduation, employment, and transfer to four-year institutions.

How Students Benefit from High-Tech, High-Wage Career Pathways

Meg Draeger

The regional Miami Valley Tech Prep Consortium (MVTPC) was formed in 1992 at Sinclair Community College (SCC) in Dayton, Ohio, as a partnership between secondary and postsecondary education and local businesses. Like other Tech Prep initiatives, it is designed to create educational pathways between high schools and community colleges in emerging career areas. MVTPC is the largest Tech Prep consortium in the state of Ohio, and one of the largest in the nation. Ten high-tech, high-wage career pathways are offered at twenty-nine secondary school program sites, enrolling more than twenty-four hundred high school juniors and seniors. In addition, more than seven hundred students have completed the secondary portion of the pathway and are currently enrolled in associate degree programs at Sinclair Community College; other students are pursuing bachelor's degrees at various other institutions. The MVTPC's (n.d.) mission is to "strengthen Ohio's workforce competitiveness by facilitating educational change to prepare students for technology-based careers" (n.p.).

The MVTPC, in conjunction with SCC, high schools, and career centers across seven counties, provides seamless career and technical education to area students. Numerous studies show the importance of community colleges in educating technology professionals (Bragg, 2003; Mattis and Sislin, 2005), and MVTPC builds on the community college's traditional strengths in career and technical education (CTE) areas. The consortium is also a participant in the College and Career Transitions Initiative (CCTI) sponsored by the League for Innovation in the Community College. This program

works to strengthen the role of community and technical colleges across the United States and to develop them into recognized leaders in career pathway preparation. Effective articulation agreements, policies and procedures, and extensive collaboration between high schools, community colleges, four-year institutions, and state higher education agencies all contribute to the success of the Tech Prep and CCTI programs in the Miami Valley region of southwest Ohio.

As the MVTPC has grown over the past thirteen years, its spectrum of education and career preparation services has evolved. Continuous monitoring of students' progression through the system and communication with instructors and counselors call attention to gaps or problems as they arise. Special programs and approaches have been developed to make sure that students with a range of backgrounds and interests can use Tech Prep to transition from high school to college, and to a meaningful career. This chapter describes a variety of activities and services provided to recruit, retain, and continually engage and motivate Tech Prep students along the pathway from early high school to college and beyond.

Student Progression Through the MVTPC Tech Prep Pathway

The MVTPC Tech Prep pathway includes activities and classes in the ninth, tenth, eleventh, and twelfth grades.

Ninth and Tenth Grades. Although Tech Prep students are officially enrolled in the program during their junior and senior years of high school, a number of events, activities, and advising sessions take place prior to the start of the junior year. One of the newest elements in the spectrum of services provided by the MVTPC is the MetaMorph Ninth Grade Career Exploration Guarantee, designed to fill a gap in career guidance identified for local ninth graders. This activity, designed by the consortium, may be considered the first step students take along a Tech Prep pathway. Through the Meta-Morph system, ninth-grade English teachers engage students in a series of Web-based activities that integrate career-awareness with Ohio language arts standards for reading, research, and writing. On completion of the prescribed sequence of activities, students design an individualized career plan and an individual education plan leading to one or two career pathways that suit them best. Guidance counselors at the high schools follow up with individual students for high school course and program selection. Some consortium high schools offer ninth-grade students a career-planning course that leads to the selection of an educational pathway and a pathway-specific tenth-grade foundations course. This class introduces students to core competencies, career opportunities, and educational opportunities in their chosen pathway.

The MVTPC, in conjunction with SCC, conducts pathway-specific "awareness days" for tenth-grade students on the college campus. These are offered halfway through the school year, when sophomores are required to enroll in Tech Prep programs. At each awareness day, the college faculty presents their programs and career fields by engaging students in hands-on demonstrations, including laboratory experiments and interactive game show formats, which allow high school students to interact with college students and MVTPC and SCC staff. Awareness days are the first organized college campus visits for potential Tech Prep students. High school instructors and counselors, as well as an increasing number of parents, accompany the tenth graders on these campus visits, which include lunch and a pathway-focused campus tour. In addition, MVTPC program managers market Tech Prep programs at open houses and recruiting events at secondary school program sites.

Eleventh and Twelfth Grades. A Tech Prep student in the MVTPC begins formal Tech Prep classes at the beginning of his or her junior year. Students' course sequence in a specific career area is complemented by rigorous academic coursework. The secondary-level coursework is generally delivered at a comprehensive high school or career center, although high school students regularly come to the college campus to participate in college-level courses in their pathway. The secondary sequence of courses is closely articulated with a sequence of courses at SCC that lead to an associate degree; in many cases, students continue along the same pathway into upper-division college coursework that leads to a bachelor's or higher degree.

To engage Tech Prep students early in the college planning process, and to allow MVTPC to track student performance, instructors are asked to have their junior students take the ACCUPLACER college placement test, which is administered at Sinclair's testing center and at some high schools. Taking the test during the junior year enables timely identification of and attention to academic weaknesses, and allows students to practice taking the exam before they must do so again in their senior year, when it functions as an actual college course placement test.

Eleventh-grade Tech Prep students, along with their instructors, are invited to the SCC campus for the consortium's junior orientation days. Like the sophomore awareness days, the MVTPC and SCC faculty and staff offer pathway-specific days during which students gain more in-depth exposure to their career pathway and the corresponding postsecondary program of study. In several pathways, a hands-on interactive demonstration or team competition is the focal point of the day.

A final opportunity for high school junior and senior students to visit the SCC campus is offered by the Tech Prep showcase competition each spring. Student teams display, present, and demonstrate class projects and compete against other teams in their program pathway. The 2005 showcase hosted more than fifty team projects. Project judges are recruited from the local professional workforce, and in teams they evaluate the projects in their respective pathway of expertise. Students are required to submit a written document about their project and prepare an oral presentation for the judges. Students must show evidence of academic and technical skills and knowledge, as well as business and industry involvement. Winning teams at the local showcase proceed to a regional showcase in which students from the four southwest Ohio Tech Prep consortia compete. On the day of the showcase, college faculty can see high school students' work firsthand, and can interact with the students and their instructors.

Ensuring Student Success Through the MVTPC Tech Prep Pathway

A variety of factors contribute to the success and retention of students in the Tech Prep pathway: MVTPC's organization and processes; the culture, operations, and commitment of faculty and staff at the secondary schools and SCC; student services; and students' familial support systems. The MVTPC works hard to help Tech Prep students and parents tap into the many resources available to them in planning and preparing for college attendance.

A defined eleventh-grade admissions standard allows provisional enrollment for a limited number of students at each secondary program site. Staff monitor provisional students' progress in remedying identified deficiencies in coursework and in raising their grade point average (GPA) to the level required for full admission to the program. MVTPC graduating seniors require approximately 50 percent less remediation in college than non-Tech Prep students of the same age.

Student Data Tracking. MVTPC, in conjunction with SCC and the secondary program sites, carefully tracks student progress through the Tech Prep pathway. Baseline student data, including GPA and academic course level and performance, are collected upon entrance into the eleventh-grade programs; Tech Prep students must be on track to successfully graduate from high school. Retention through the secondary portion of the program is tracked by noting high school graduation, performance in technical courses, and GPA at graduation. Additional data include matriculation and enrollment at postsecondary institutions, the amount of remedial course work required, and degrees and certificates earned. MVTPC also tracks student persistence in college; students are considered successful when they complete sixty or more hours of nondevelopmental college credit toward a degree.

Data tracking allows identification of opportunities to improve system performance. A combination of information systems is employed to track consortium data, including manual data collection and documentation at the high school sites, local consortium databases, college databases, and state agency databases such as Ohio's Higher Education Information system. Most MVTPC interventions and established practices described in this chapter arose in response to program weaknesses identified by data. For example, having students engage in multiple retakes of the ACCUPLACER college placement exam, beginning in junior year, came about because the students did not generally perform well the first time they took it, no matter which courses they had completed. Focused professional development for math teachers grew out of identified deficiencies in student preparation for college-level technical math courses (see the following section for more on this).

College Partnership. The MVTPC's success depends on college faculty as well as the collaboration and cooperation of numerous SCC departments, including divisional academic advising, the assessment and intake center, the career planning and placement center, financial aid, admissions, the experience-based education office, student records, and institutional planning and research. Students and parents are repeatedly reminded of the need to file the Free Application for Federal Student Aid (FAFSA) to ensure eligibility for the SCC Tech Prep scholarship and any other potential funding opportunities. Career guidance and transition programs address financial planning for college as an integral part of the career exploration process. The MetaMorph ninth-grade program also includes lessons on the financial aspects of continuing education.

The Sinclair Tech Prep scholarship, initiated in 1994 by the college's board of directors, creates an incentive for high school Tech Prep graduates to continue their education at SCC. Additional financial scholarships are available for students transferring from SCC to the University of Dayton, a private Catholic university located less than five miles from Sinclair. Several specific pathways offer a dual admission agreement, with guaranteed acceptance into the university as a junior, and partial tuition scholarships offered to students who satisfactorily complete high school Tech Prep and associate degree programs. This is an incentive for high school students to plan for a bachelor's degree via a Tech Prep pathway while still in high school.

Per national Tech Prep guidelines, both male and female students are encouraged to consider career areas not traditionally popular for their gender. SCC offers many gender- or culture-specific programs, services, and scholarship opportunities, such as women in engineering technologies, Appalachian students, Hispanic students, and first-generation college students. Collaboration with the college organizations responsible for these initiatives (for example, Women in Engineering Technologies Association) allows an increasing number of nontraditional students to successfully complete postsecondary CTE. Although female high school enrollment in traditionally single-sex career fields, such as engineering and allied health technologies, remains low, the MVTPC and SCC assist high schools in recruiting specific groups of students to reduce the discrepancies.

Once in college, SCC offers Tech Prep students access to small classes and individualized attention by faculty and staff. Technical faculty and academic advisors remain abreast of the students' performance in all coursework, and when necessary, make adjustments to students' course-load or refer them to the academic resource center's individualized computer tutorials, peer tutoring, or academic support services. For example, the college assists engineering technology students with mathematics coursework by offering a 100-level technical mathematics course in two formats. Students can choose between a traditional lecture format or a combination lecture and hands-on lab model. Many Tech Prep students are more successful and more motivated in the lab environment, because it provides a continuation of the teaching and learning styles used in Tech Prep high school programs.

Across most degree preparation programs at SCC, hands-on and project- and competency-based teaching and learning are evident, in part because of the growing interface between Tech Prep and secondary CTE programs. Every one of the six academic divisions at SCC is involved in at least one of the ten MVTPC career pathways. This facilitates institution-wide transition toward Tech Prep modes of teaching and learning. The MVTPC invites an increasing number of college faculty to participate in events aimed at building collaboration between high school and college instructors. As Tech Prep student success is better monitored and communicated, college faculty and staff are more willing to believe in the program and to go out of their way to cooperate with high schools and other Tech Prep programs.

Faculty Professional Development and Support

To facilitate smooth transitions for students between high school and college, as well as to ensure curriculum alignment, ongoing collaboration among faculty is essential. The MVTPC facilitates collaboration in several ways. First, high school and college instructors from each program pathway convene annually for an instructor summit at SCC. This is an invaluable opportunity for high school teachers from different schools to network with each other, and the event fosters two-way communication between high school and college faculty. Faculty and staff present relevant updates about college course articulation procedures, college course content, and news about upcoming student or instructor events. In most cases, instructors can participate in a brief in-service training that addresses a current topic in their career pathway, such as spreadsheet applications for engineering technology. The instructor summits are conducted each fall, during a school day, and the consortium offers to compensate school districts for substitute costs.

Academic Focus. In 2002, to address an increasing emphasis on academic rigor and applied academics in CTE pathways, the MVTPC established a contextual integrated academic leadership team for each pathway. The teams were made up of instructors from the various secondary program sites, including a technical teacher, an English or language arts teacher, a math teacher, a science teacher, and a guidance counselor. A series of professional development workshops was conducted for each team across a two-year period with the intention that those team members would serve as trainers for broadening the focus on rigorous, integrated curricula to all program sites.

By 2004, the approach to integrating curriculum had changed somewhat. At this time, there was a need for a greater focus on the academic areas of emphasis in each pathway. Because of the significance of math to the engineering technology pathway, a math instructional leadership team was formed to provide specific professional development and interaction with college faculty and staff. This team is still in place, and addresses such topics as ACCUPLACER test performance monitoring, and improvement and alignment between high school and college math courses. When the teams formed, many high school math instructors had never personally taken the ACCUPLACER test, so that was one of the first orders of business.

The math leadership team aims to eliminate the need for remedial math upon college enrollment and to improve student readiness for college math coursework. Ongoing relationships and communication between high school math and technical teachers and college faculty is critical to achieve this goal. A similar team development process will be initiated for English and language arts instructors. This model of academic leadership teams in each career pathway will be replicated across all pathways in the consortium.

Faculty Professional Development. The consortium's Teachers in Industry for Educational Support program is another unique opportunity for teachers. The three-week summer externship program was started in 1996, and has involved more than seventy-five business partners and four hundred K–12 teachers, primarily secondary math, science, and technical instructors. Teams of teachers are assigned to a single worksite according to their subject areas. Business partners work with the MVTPC program coordinator to design relevant projects for the teams. The teams are then responsible for completing an industry-specific work assignment and developing and documenting a related interdisciplinary applied curriculum unit. A MVTPC staff member conducts a worksite visit during the last week of the program, and each educator team presents a summary of its project and curriculum at a concluding workshop held at SCC for educator and business partner participants.

Counselor Professional Development. Because high school guidance counselors are critical in the recruitment and retention of students in career pathways, the MVTPC devotes significant effort to collaborating with them and providing the resources necessary to advise their students. In addition, a twelfth-grade guidance counselor summit is conducted each spring that focuses on transitioning students to college. Counselors review procedures for claiming college credit earned in the secondary portion of the program, as well as Tech Prep scholarship specifics and college admissions and registration processes.

College Faculty and Staff Professional Development. In addition to high school and college instructors and guidance counselors, there is a designated group of Tech Prep pathway coordinators who are college faculty, department chairs, or deans. Participants in this group convene each fall to learn about new consortium procedures, new or developing pathways, new high school program sites, and performance of the previous year's high school graduating class of Tech Prep students. This group plans on-campus student events, such as the awareness days and orientation days.

Business Partnerships. The consortium encourages both high school and college instructors to create tangible connections between students and the workplace in the form of job shadowing experiences, mock interviews, résumé workshops, internships or co-ops, mentor relationships for student projects, and facilitation of in-class or in-lab hands-on learning activities. Representatives from local businesses regularly serve on industrial advisory committees for pathway programs and participate in curriculum development and revision. They also help validate program quality and relevance and foster public relations and marketing of career pathways and occupations.

Additional MVTPC Resources. The MVTPC makes available a range of print and online resources. Pathway outline sheets, detailed career pathway templates of the specific course sequences for grades 9 to 14, articulation agreements between high schools and SCC, curricular courses of study for each pathway, links to high school and college programs, and procedural references for instructors and administrators are just some of the resources available online. The MVTPC staff makes yearly fall visits to each secondary program site to hand-deliver an annually updated consortium resource manual and review current programs, procedures, and calendars of events.

Conclusion

We are all engaged in preparing today's students to participate successfully in tomorrow's workforce, which may include high-tech jobs that have not yet been defined. Students, as well as the organizations that serve them by delivering Tech Prep and CTE, need to continually develop by expanding their frame of reference for processing new information and knowledge. Relationships between abstract concepts and practical applications need to be continuously reinforced for students by the educational team of faculty and business partners. Students need to distinguish among multiple occupations within single career fields, and recognize and gain transferable skills across those fields. Employers need to be engaged to design and deliver education and career preparation so that workforce needs are met. A solid preparation in the basics—reading, writing, and arithmetic—remains indispensable in secondary and postsecondary education, along with the ability to think critically, systematically, creatively, and collaboratively. SCC and the MVTPC employ those same skills in designing and delivering effective high school, college, and career transition programs.

References

Bragg, D. D. *Case Study Report: Sinclair Community College, College and Career Transition Initiative.* Phoenix: League for Innovation in the Community College, 2003.

Mattis, M. C., and Sislin, J. (eds.). *Enhancing the Community College Pathway to Engineering Careers.* Washington, D.C.: National Academies Press, 2005.

Miami Valley Tech Prep Consortium. *About.* Dayton, Ohio: Sinclair Community College, Miami Valley Tech Prep Consortium, n.d. http://www.mvtechprep.org/about/about.htm. Accessed May 22, 2006.

MEG DRAEGER is program manager for engineering technologies with the Miami Valley Tech Prep Consortium at Sinclair Community College in Dayton, Ohio.

9

Future teachers must be more than highly qualified; they must also be highly effective. The state of Arizona is proactively developing partnerships that will ensure that future teachers are ready for the rigorous expectations of the profession. These partnerships have created teacher education pathways that link high schools, community colleges, and public universities.

Arizona's Teacher Education Initiative: Aligning High School and College Curricula

Cheri St. Arnauld

In the past several years, institutions of higher education have been criticized for the poor preparation and quality of new teachers, and policymakers have challenged the entire educational system to work together to create new pathways to prepare teachers. The K–12 community has struggled with differing expectations for teacher credentials, as well as the public's perception that students are not always taught by highly qualified instructors. Indeed, in the United States teacher attrition is high, dropout rates are high, and students score lower in math and science than their peers around the world. These concerns also ring true in Arizona, where teacher shortages exist in rural, urban, and suburban areas, especially in special education, mathematics, and science. Although progress is being made, Arizona continues to report one of the highest dropout rates and lowest levels of student achievement in the nation.

In response to demand from K–12 partners for greater numbers of teachers, community colleges in Arizona began developing teacher preparation programs on a larger scale in 2000. Sporadic individual partnerships had previously been developed between individual campuses and universities, but most of these efforts were disparate and uncoordinated. By 2000 all sectors of the state education system were required to work together, aligning efforts across the educational continuum to increase teacher numbers and quality. This chapter describes the efforts of the National Center for Teacher Education at the Maricopa Community Colleges to implement a

statewide career pathway for preparing future teachers through the alignment of programs, policies, and curricula.

Arizona's Teacher Education Initiatives

The Maricopa Community Colleges comprise ten nationally accredited two-year colleges, two skill centers, and numerous campuses, educational centers, and teaching sites. The colleges educate and train more than 275,000 credit and noncredit students every year. Each of the ten colleges has a unique teacher preparation program that meets different community and student needs, and each college functions autonomously in the college system. Until 2001 there was little discussion among the colleges about systemwide implementation of teacher education. The National Center for Teacher Education, a new department in the Maricopa Community Colleges' Academic Affairs division, was created to develop multifaceted initiatives and programs intended to improve the recruitment, preparation, and retention of future K–12 teachers.

The National Center for Teacher Education's first initiative, called the Teacher Education Partnership Commission (TEPC; www.teacherpartner. com), is cochaired by the center's director and the superintendent of the Liberty School District. The TEPC is made up of forty K–12, community college, university, business, government, and community leaders from Maricopa County, but has recently expanded to include other community colleges and universities in the state. It is designed to improve communication, influence policy, and develop programs to alleviate the teacher shortage in Arizona. The TEPC, which meets once a month, provides a forum for partners to develop a shared vision of teacher preparation. TEPC partners discuss and develop consensus about many current educational issues in Arizona. The group has learned to speak with one voice, and has issued two consensus briefs, titled *Characteristics of a Quality Teacher* (2003) and *Quality Teacher Preparation Programs* (2005). TEPC was one of the first places in Arizona where two- and four-year institutions could discuss how best to develop articulated, high-quality programs.

The National Center for Teacher Education also supports the National Association of Community College Teacher Education Programs (NACCTEP; www.nacctep.org), formed in partnership with the League for Innovation in the Community College and the American Association of Community Colleges. This association provides leadership and support for community colleges across the nation that are involved in teacher education. NACCTEP began in 2002 and currently has more than five hundred members from forty states. The director of the National Center for Teacher Education also serves as the executive director of NACCTEP.

The National Center for Teacher Education's third project is the College and Career Transition Initiative (CCTI), a partnership between Maricopa Community Colleges, the League for Innovation in the Community

NEW DIRECTIONS FOR COMMUNITY COLLEGES • DOI: 10.1002/cc

College, and the Office of Vocational and Adult Education at the U.S. Department of Education. This initiative involves fifteen community colleges that are developing articulated pathways in several career clusters. Maricopa Community Colleges was chosen as one of three sites to develop a career pathway in teacher education. Both TEPC and NACCTEP were new initiatives when the CCTI project started, which provided an opportunity to merge, mutually support, and align these initiatives to build quality pathways.

In keeping with the mission of the National Center of Teacher Education, the Maricopa Community Colleges' CCTI partnership focuses on developing a coherent sequence of rigorous courses, and refines practices that help students move effectively from high school to college and on to careers in education by better aligning secondary and postsecondary programs in teacher preparation. This initiative was designed to support the principles outlined in the 2001 federal No Child Left Behind (NCLB) legislation by investing in strategies that close the achievement gap between poor and minority students and their white and more affluent peers. CCTI also creates meaningful educational options to help students from diverse backgrounds reach uniformly high standards, and ensures that students continue to attain these high standards at each level of their educational careers.

CCTI's desired student outcomes include decreased need for remediation at the postsecondary level, increased enrollment and persistence in postsecondary education, increased academic and skill achievement at the secondary and postsecondary levels, increased attainment of postsecondary degrees, certificates, or other recognized credentials, and increased entry into employment.

CCTI Project Partners

To better support the CCTI project, the National Center for Teacher Education aligned itself with other initiatives and educational efforts influencing Arizona's educational environment in order to draw on resources and take advantage of other policy efforts focused on increasing the quality of teacher preparation. The CCTI project originally included three of Maricopa's ten colleges: Estrella Mountain Community College, South Mountain Community College, and Phoenix College. Each works with a high school partner to identify a cohort of high school students to participate in the project and all three aim to achieve the outcomes identified in the CCTI grant.

For the CCTI project, Estrella Mountain Community College developed a traditional two-plus-two articulated course sequence with Peoria Unified School District. Peoria is the third largest school district in Arizona, serving over thirty-six thousand students. Five of the six Peoria high schools are participating in this project. They provide a high-quality articulated teacher education pathway in cooperation with Estrella Mountain Community College and have worked closely with the institution to identify specific strategies that help students transition and progress through the education system.

Phoenix College took an alternative approach and established a relationship with Teacher Prep Charter High School, an institution specifically created in 2003 to educate future teachers. The purpose of Teacher Prep Charter High School is to prepare high school students for entry into college-level teacher education programs. Similarly, South Mountain Community College is working toward a partnership with the Achieving a College Education (ACE) program based at a nearby high school. The ACE program recruits students during their sophomore year. Once accepted, these students begin taking college classes in the summer, then attend college classes on Saturdays during their junior and senior years in high school. Students in the ACE program take college courses while still enrolled in their high school and transfer their college credits to the community college after graduation.

CCTI Project Design

Several issues facing the college system have affected the CCTI project design. Each of the three colleges participating in the program was in varying stages of implementing teacher preparation programs when the initiative began. In addition, each college had its own programmatic transfer agreements with the public university. Furthermore, one university has three separate campuses; each one had a different entrance requirement for incoming teacher education students. Students could not be assured that the teacher preparation classes they had taken would transfer from one college campus to another. To develop a coherent, articulated teacher education pathway, the community colleges and university system needed to undertake a policy review. Systemwide articulation was needed between institutions, between programs, and between the faculty and teachers at the various institutions. The CCTI project thus focused on aligning institutions and curricula, reviewing policies, and improving communication among various professionals about quality teacher preparation. The alignment between initiatives is one of the strengths of the CCTI project, and has positively affected the state's ability to effectively train future teachers. Furthermore, although only three of Maricopa's ten colleges are formally involved in the CCTI project, its principles and strategies are interwoven in the work of the National Center for Teacher Education and its many initiatives, and affect the entire Maricopa Community College system.

Policy Alignment

Arizona's first and strongest effort to improve the preparation of future teachers in Arizona was the development of the associate of arts in elementary education (AAEE) degree. This degree requires completion of sixty to sixty-three semester credits in general education and teacher education coursework, is designed for both paraprofessionals and transfer students, and has been offered at all community colleges in the state since fall 2003. The first two years of the degree program are designed for students who plan to transfer to an elementary or special education program at an Arizona university or who plan to become a classroom instructional aide. They include courses required for general education, education foundation courses, and specific electives that meet the Arizona Professional Teacher Standards. The AAEE degree and all its credits transfer as a block to any of Arizona's public universities, and successful completion of the AAEE degree meets general requirements for admission to any of the public universities. In addition, the AAEE degree provides students with the knowledge necessary for Arizona's state licensure exam, the Arizona Educator Proficiency Assessment. Completion of the AAEE degree also provides students with the skills and direct classroom experience necessary to be deemed "highly qualified" under NCLB legislation. (Further information on the AAEE degree can be accessed at http://www.teach.maricopa.edu/.)

The AAEE degree solved many of the alignment problems that existed between the state's community colleges and universities, and is the policy framework on which all other alignment discussions were built. Currently, work is under way to develop and implement an associate of arts degree in secondary education by fall 2006.

Another statewide effort that became a policy foundation for Arizona's teacher education initiative started at the Arizona Department of Education's Career and Technical Education (CTE) division, and is a high school CTE curriculum to serve future K–12 teachers. Three Arizona Department of Education divisions—the career technical division, the exceptional student division, and the academic support division—came together to fund a new program called Education Professions. This program, fashioned after South Carolina's Teacher Cadet Program, identifies cohorts of high school students who want to become teachers, and is designed to prepare secondary students for employment or postsecondary opportunities in education. The program's curriculum is available to juniors and seniors across the state.

The Education Professions curriculum provides instruction in education career choices, education structure and systems, theory, pedagogy, developmental stages, learning styles, and methodology. In addition to technical skills, students completing this program develop advanced critical thinking skills, enhanced academic skills, and a greater sense of civic responsibility. They also begin to understand education as consumers and to develop employability and leadership skills. The program employs a delivery system composed of four integral parts: formal or technical instruction, experiential or service learning, supervised work-based learning, and participation in a student organization called Future Educators of America. The program also provides interactive classroom experiences with students at different age levels and in a variety of content areas. The curriculum framework for Education Professions can be accessed at the Arizona Tech Prep Web site (http://www.aztechprep.org). Currently, 948 students in sixty-two Arizona schools participate in the Education Professions program.

The National Center for Teacher Education and the Education Professions program have developed a strong partnership that is the foundation for the career pathway used in the CCTI project. This pathway integrates the secondary Education Professions curriculum framework and course requirements for the AAEE statewide degree program. Students enrolled in this pathway can transfer to any public university in the state, as well as some private universities. Students in the Education Professions program can also participate in dual and concurrent enrollment opportunities at community colleges. High school dual enrollment students can take the introduction to education course in the AAEE degree program, as well as other paraprofessional certificate and degree courses. They can also take English, math, and science dual enrollment courses. Developing policy frameworks that allowed these two programs to align systemically across the state was the first step in developing a quality teacher education pathway from high school through the baccalaureate.

Program Alignment

Once the policies and pathways necessary to align a rigorous sequence of coursework were complete, the National Center for Teacher Education began convening teachers and faculty to align curricula across programs and to implement the goals of the CCTI project. The National Center for Teacher Education supported two critical analyses that guaranteed program alignment. The first was a comparative analysis designed to assess whether the competencies necessary to complete the Education Professions high school curriculum were aligned with the knowledge needed to succeed in education foundation courses in the AAEE degree. This analysis supported dual enrollment efforts and built an extra measure of quality control into articulation agreements being established by community colleges and the Arizona Department of Education through the Education Professions curriculum. The second critical piece of work was an analysis of the alignment between the AAEE degree and Arizona's licensure exam, the Educator Proficiency Assessment. This project ensured that students receiving their first two years of higher education at the community college would be prepared to pass the state licensure exam. Both of these analyses helped ensure quality and credibility to rapidly expanding teacher education programs at the high schools and community colleges.

The National Center for Teacher Education also examined the alignment of Arizona's high-stakes graduation test with entrance requirements for college courses. This analysis, completed by community college faculty, revealed that the two were not aligned, and in fact, the high school graduation exam and the content covered in community college courses had few

NEW DIRECTIONS FOR COMMUNITY COLLEGES • DOI: 10.1002/cc

similarities. Further work and analysis will be required to develop ways to bridge the educational systems to create seamless transitions for students.

Student Support

The next step in aligning Arizona's teacher education programs involved supporting efforts at both the college and program levels to strengthen students' academic skills. The following strategies proved successful in helping Arizona students transition through the state's teacher education pathway.

Early Assessment. The CCTI project includes expectations for early assessments, advising, and additional preparation to ensure student success and persistence. CCTI students enrolled in the Education Professions high school program take the ACCUPLACER assessment exam for community college course placement in the eleventh or twelfth grade. This exam is usually administered during the first semester of enrollment in the program, but it can be retaken in the senior year. Students receive their scores on this online exam (as well as potential course placement information) immediately, and depending on their scores, are counseled and advised about options for additional support.

Individualized College and Career Plans. Using early assessment information from the ACCUPLACER test, each student works with faculty and advisers from both high schools and community colleges to develop an individualized college and career plan. The plan provides a framework for meeting individual students' academic needs and career education goals, and lays out a rigorous sequence of academic coursework. The plan also addresses financial aid information, early assessment results, educational philosophy, and career planning. Once developed, the high school and college partnership team of faculty and advisers determines the resources necessary to meet the needs of each student. Students are offered tutoring, remedial or advanced coursework, dual enrollment, and other educational opportunities. Individualized college and career plans are first created at the high school level, but move with students as they transition between institutions. Students in the CCTI project use electronic portfolios that demonstrate competencies mastered throughout the program.

Future Teachers Clubs. Maricopa's CCTI project works closely with future teachers clubs from partner high schools and community colleges. These clubs provide students with opportunities to explore careers in education, gain a realistic understanding of the role of the teacher, and encourage students from diverse backgrounds to think seriously about the teaching profession. All of the CCTI partner schools have future teachers clubs, and two high schools—Peoria High School and Sunrise Mountain High School—are internationally recognized Future Educators of America charter chapters. Future teachers club activities for high school students can include community service projects (such as donation drives, judging an elementary school science fair, or manning a booth at a school or local event) and professional development opportunities such as listening to guest speakers, portfolio training, and opportunities to visit and participate in local schools. Involvement in these clubs develops students' leadership skills and creates a sense of community for future teachers. Additional CCTI funding has supported future teachers conferences, and a partnership with the Phoenix Suns, the professional basketball team in Arizona, has involved over 750 high school and community college students in club activities. The Phoenix Suns support future teacher preparation by offering use of their facilities, tickets to games, and guest speakers. Conferences are held in the spring and fall and provide students with career, higher education, and professional opportunities.

Electronic Portfolios. The e-portfolio component of the CCTI program is used by project high schools, community colleges, and universities involved in preparing future teachers in Arizona. The goal is to promote high-quality dialogue among teachers and faculty related to strengthening the learning process, building authentic assessment, and demonstrating mastery of competencies. The high school Education Professions program, the community college system, and several university systems serving CCTI students have all chosen to use the same e-portfolio in their teacher preparation programs.

The e-portfolio also allows secondary and postsecondary faculty to receive group and individual professional development training. The portfolio provides Web-based tools for K–12 learning communities and teacher education communities. CCTI secondary and postsecondary faculty also use the e-portfolio to create portfolio templates and assess students' portfolios online. It can be used as well to create and share standards-based lessons and units, including assessment rubrics. The Web Folio Builder makes it easy for students to create, organize, and share electronic portfolios. In addition, several Arizona K–12 student districts are implementing the e-portfolio as a lesson-planning tool.

The goal of the e-portfolio effort is to develop a continuum of electronic portfolios to be shared among high schools, community colleges, and universities, as well as places of employment. This effort will allow for the progressive growth and assessment of students' knowledge and skills, and can become a catalyst for continued dialogue among faculty.

Conclusion

Curriculum and competency alignment across institutions is key to a successful career pathway. However, without total buy-in from all stakeholders, alignment will not be a systemic improvement. The Education Professions program and the statewide AAEE degree were developed independently of one another. The Arizona Department of Education included postsecondary representatives in the development of the Education Professions program, and thus it was designed to articulate with the introductory courses offered in other postsecondary teacher education programs in Arizona. However, before the CCTI project, the Department of Education did not seek formal articulation or dual enrollment agreements.

In contrast, the AAEE degree was developed with the buy-in of all Arizona's institutions of higher education, and formal articulation agreements among these institutions were established from the start. Although many of the same individuals participated in both the Education Professions and AAEE development processes, the projects were not vertically aligned. The CCTI project became the catalyst that pushed the Maricopa Community Colleges and the Arizona Department of Education to work together to develop a career pathway spanning the two programs. Without such a catalyst, the two programs may never have been integrated into a seamless pathway.

Maricopa also learned that support systems for students, parents, faculty, and academic advisers must be in place if a career pathway is to be successful. Each institution must identify the role it will play in student success and persistence, and all institutions must continuously cooperate to identify ways to work together to ensure that students' needs are met. Furthermore, Maricopa learned that data-sharing barriers between partners implementing career pathways must be eliminated; student data and tracking systems are essential to the success of a career pathway. All stakeholders (students, parents, faculty, advisers, and administrators) must understand the value of using data to support and retain students in the career pathway. When possible, existing institutional data collection systems should be integrated into shared systems instead of being duplicated or re-created.

Community colleges are uniquely positioned to work with both secondary schools and four-year colleges and universities, and have strong relationships with businesses and educational service agencies in the communities they serve. The career pathway model requires a seamless, systemic approach that supports communication between faculty and services for students through e-portfolio training, assessment, and content applications. Strong articulation agreements between high schools and community colleges—and between community colleges and four-year institutions—are necessary for students to persist in and progress through teacher education pathways.

Finally, Maricopa learned that each institution participating in a teacher education career pathway—whether it is implemented at a local, state, or national level—must identify a strong, committed leader who can become a champion for the pathway and support it with all available resources. Where possible, these leaders must integrate the goals and strategies of the career pathway into the mission, vision, and practices of their institution. Only this kind of integration can ensure a systemic and sustainable teacher education career pathway.

NEW DIRECTIONS FOR COMMUNITY COLLEGES • DOI: 10.1002/cc

References

Teacher Education Partnership Commission. *Characteristics of a Quality Teacher.* Tempe, Ariz.: Maricopa Community Colleges, National Center for Teacher Education, 2003.
Teacher Education Partnership Commission. *Quality Teacher Preparation Programs: Pre K–12.* Tempe, Ariz.: Maricopa Community Colleges, National Center for Teacher Education, 2005.

CHERI ST. ARNAULD is national director of teacher education programs for Maricopa Community Colleges in Phoenix, Arizona.

10

Drawing on previous chapters in the volume, this chapter identifies crosscutting themes and lessons for those engaged in the development and study of academic pathways. Particular attention is paid to the ways that pathways can increase opportunities for traditionally underserved students.

Academic Pathways and Increased Opportunities for Underserved Students: Crosscutting Themes and Lessons Learned

Elisabeth A. Barnett, Debra D. Bragg

This volume presents a wide array of models and perspectives on academic pathways that create opportunities for students to enter and succeed in progressively higher levels of education. Academic pathways—defined as boundary-spanning curricula, instructional approaches, and organizational structures—are increasingly prevalent in the United States, the result of heightened concerns about the progression of all students through the existing P–16 (preschool through sixteenth grade) system. Some established, some emerging, academic pathways are creating increasingly varied and propitious routes to and through college, potentially allowing students who may not fit the profile of a traditional college-goer to flourish in higher education. Drawing on findings and examples from previous chapters in the volume, this chapter identifies crosscutting themes and perspectives and highlights lessons for those involved in developing or studying academic pathways to and from the community college.

Multiple Pathways and Opportunities

Creating multiple academic pathways to higher education and careers can play a key role in opening doors to postsecondary education for traditionally underserved students. Some students respond well to the concrete

learning and job-related rewards associated with career and technical education (see Chapter Seven), whereas others are attracted to small, personalized educational opportunities, such as the middle and early college high schools discussed in Chapter Five. Students who are bored in high school may become engaged in their education through opportunities to participate in dual enrollment or by attending school on a college campus, whereas others may flourish by engaging in experiential learning that yields college credit, such as career-related internships and externships. Furthermore, distance learning can broaden the range of courses available to students, especially those living in remote rural areas, and can become an academic pathway in and of itself, as discussed in Chapter One.

As well, multiple entry and exit points to the educational pipeline offer students more options and greater flexibility than the traditional college preparatory curriculum. As Chapter Two illustrates, underserved students often are not exposed to a college preparatory pathway at the eighth- or ninth-grade level, which reduces their ability to take advantage of accelerated learning opportunities such as AP and dual credit. Programs such as Tech Prep and those that bridge the GED to a college curriculum provide a greater number of students—including those who may not have considered college to be an option—with multiple points of entry to higher education.

Lesson: Educators and policymakers should establish systems that provide multiple pathways to college and careers in order to meet students' diverse needs and interests.

Overlapping and Integrated Academic Pathways

Over the years, many academic pathways have achieved success by adopting elements from earlier or similar programs. For example, the early college high school evolved from middle college high schools established in the 1970s. Other pathways have integrated several previously disparate elements. College Tech Prep, for example, integrates CTE with the traditional college preparatory pathway. These and other academic pathways are built on dual credit programs, or use dual credit policies and mechanisms in order to accelerate student progress through the education system. As well, distance education programs are often integrated with other academic pathways, such as Tech Prep, AP, and International Baccalaureate (IB), as discussed in Chapter One.

High Schools That Work and the College and Career Transitions Initiative (CCTI; see Chapters Seven, Eight, and Nine) also integrate a number of academic pathways. Besides extensive use of dual credit, they incorporate a Tech Prep design that includes a college preparatory curriculum. In addition, several of their local sites have developed bridge programs that are available to students in the summer months. Similarly, some early college high schools incorporate GED options that bridge to college, Tech Prep curricula, or AP courses. By integrating elements of many different academic pathways to college, educators strengthen existing programs and build on the successes of others.

New Directions for Community Colleges • DOI: 10.1002/cc

Lesson: Consider developing new pathways that build on existing ones, and that can take advantage of established agreements, local knowledge, and practical experience with the creation of academic pathways to college.

Spanning Multiple Levels of the P–16 System

Some academic pathways, such as Advanced Placement (AP) and dual credit, connect high school to two- or four-year colleges, allowing high school students to begin college-level coursework when they demonstrate competency, and aligning the high school and college curriculum, often in career and technical education (CTE) areas. Recently, academic pathways have begun to link the programs and credentials of high schools, community colleges, and four-year institutions; these frequently involve both curricular and organizational restructuring. For example, the community college baccalaureate, discussed in detail in Chapter Six, provides community college students with access to bachelor's degrees in applied programs that four-year institutions frequently do not offer. Similarly, formal articulation agreements that span educational systems, such as those discussed in Chapters Eight and Nine, allow students to begin a program of study in high school and progress seamlessly through three or more institutions to earn a bachelor's or other advanced degree. To facilitate transition, some programs simultaneously admit students into two-year and four-year colleges.

Underserved students are likely to benefit from these pathways for several reasons. First, they can lower college costs considerably, especially in models that allow students to earn dual credit while still in high school (see Chapter Four). Through extra guidance and mentorship from instructors, counselors, and other academic personnel, these pathways may also help students develop a greater commitment to attaining a postsecondary credential. Often, academic pathways provide underserved students, who may have little experience with higher education, with greater confidence in their ability to navigate a complex, multilayered educational system (see Chapter Five for examples of how students benefit from participating in a boundary-spanning academic pathway).

Lesson: Where possible and appropriate, pathways that span multiple levels of the education system should be established. They provide opportunities for students to advance their education by providing clear and well-marked routes to higher levels of educational attainment.

The Lead Role of Career and Technical Education (CTE)

As discussed in Chapter Seven, several of the earliest academic pathways involved CTE, and some of its most important features have been widely adopted. Academic pathways that integrate CTE often implement new curricular and instructional approaches that motivate students to stay in high school and matriculate to college. For example, the integrated and contextual learning approaches emphasized in High Schools That Work and Project Lead the Way, both described in Chapter Seven, emphasize instructional practices that make learning more relevant and engaging for students. Educators developing and supporting other academic pathways can learn much from these and other CTE programs.

In addition, academic pathways that integrate CTE tend to clearly emphasize a goal linked to employment, which is extremely important to many students. For example, students who engage in Tech Prep or the CCTI program (see Chapters Eight and Nine) know that they are obtaining the competencies and credentials that will help them prepare for their career. Compared to the sometimes harder to visualize goals associated with general education, academic pathways that incorporate CTE offer tangible educational and labor market rewards that are attractive to students and can motivate them to persist in their education.

Lesson: Career and technical education programs have important experiences and useful curricula, instructional methods, and materials to share with those engaged in the development of new academic pathways. These approaches may be especially important in meeting the needs of traditionally underserved students.

Beyond the Curriculum: The Role of Student Support

A number of chapters in this volume have acknowledged that although curricular change is important, extensive student support systems are needed if academic pathways are to be effective mechanisms for providing opportunities for underserved students to enter and succeed in college. In some cases, special efforts are needed to ensure that students learn about different pathways and view them as viable options. For example, as several of the authors in this volume point out, many high school students do not know where the nearest college campus is located and do not understand what will be required of them in college courses. Opportunities that allow students to spend time on a campus, get to know faculty and staff, explore the facilities, and engage in hands-on activities are extremely valuable. These opportunities should be strategically structured at different grade levels and stages of the educational process.

Furthermore, as discussed in Chapter Two, the climate of the school, as well as teacher attitudes and assumptions about student ability, can greatly affect student success in an academic pathway. In some cases, teacher dispositions can be influenced through professional development seminars and involvement in faculty-driven projects, such as those discussed in Chapter Three. When executed successfully, professional development can bring teachers together to examine their own practices and develop new ways of thinking about their teaching philosophies and practices to improve student outcomes. Educational structures such as block scheduling, integrated curricula, and opportunities for extra help can also help improve student experiences in academic pathways.

Lesson: Pathways can play an important role in helping traditionally underserved students enter and succeed in college. However, thoughtfully designed supports are needed to ensure that students fully benefit from these opportunities.

The Signaling Role of Academic Pathways

In Chapter Three, Andrea Bueschel and Andrea Venezia point out the perplexing paradox of open access institutions: they send signals that encourage students to matriculate but at the same time convey that preparation for college is not critical. Many students who enter community colleges have absorbed this mixed message, and as a result are unprepared for the demands of college-level instruction and must take remedial and developmental classes before they can progress to the college-level curriculum. Academic pathways help communicate a college's academic expectations in concrete ways.

Lesson: The signaling role of academic pathways should not be underestimated. Schools and colleges should explore ways to use pathways to help students understand what is involved in preparing for college, and what will be expected of them upon matriculation.

Student Assessments and Academic Pathways

The movement toward competency-based, and more recently, outcomes-based measures of college readiness has gained momentum over the past decade or two, encouraging institutions to assess whether and how students are progressing along an academic pathway. Although fraught with controversy, standardized assessments are increasingly used to determine whether students have achieved success at each level and whether they are ready to move to the next. This information may also be used by high schools to make sure that students are adequately prepared for college before they enroll, and to allow schools to adjust their curricula, instruction, and student supports accordingly.

Lesson: Assessments associated with academic pathways provide important information about whether schools are adequately preparing students for college-level course work. Furthermore, assessments can help schools and colleges target extra assistance to students in pathways who are not meeting key benchmarks.

Pathways and System Alignment

High school and community college curricula become misaligned for many reasons. Traditionally, K–12 and higher education systems have communicated very little with one another. Furthermore, high school teachers are generally expected to help students meet the standards required for high school graduation, rather than those necessary to enter and succeed in college. Similarly, colleges are not always proactive in conveying their standards and expectations to entering students—or to high school counselors, teachers, and administrators. Additional complications are introduced by the lack of communication between different postsecondary institutions in states (or across the nation), which results in a lack of consensus on the meaning of "college readiness." Finally, both high school and college faculty work in relative isolation, often with few opportunities to examine how their syllabi and instructional practices align with those used by others.

Academic pathways can play a role in addressing these and other alignment issues. At the local level, establishing academic pathways leads to dialogues among those at the secondary and postsecondary levels that produce greater awareness of mismatched curricula and instructional practices. Awareness alone can be helpful, but as several chapters in this volume have pointed out, explicit efforts must also be made to increase alignment. This generally involves working collaboratively with professionals at other levels of the education system to analyze and improve curricula, instruction, and assessment policies and practices

Lesson: The creation of academic pathways can lead to productive discussions about overall system alignment. At the local level, cross-institutional faculty discussions about overlaps and gaps in the curriculum can be helpful. State-level discussions should emphasize policy change and statewide alignment efforts.

Changing Power Dynamics in the P–16 System

As academic pathways expand and develop, they sometimes bring to light competing interests—and issues of power and control—in the educational system. In particular, the postsecondary system has historically been stratified, with research universities and private colleges at the top of the hierarchy and community colleges near the bottom. The ability of academic pathways to reach their full potential often depends to a significant degree on the willingness of those at higher levels of the system to cooperate with those at lower levels. For example, AP, IB, and dual enrollment credits have little value unless they are accepted at the colleges and universities where students matriculate. Similarly, faculty have traditionally had a high level of control over course content, especially at the postsecondary level. Although this may be necessary to create an atmosphere of learning and investigation that is free of external constraints and pressures, college faculty may have few incentives to work with high school teachers to discuss ways to improve student instruction.

Recently, some of the traditional relationships between institutions and people in the secondary and postsecondary sectors have changed, partially in response to the need to improve student progress along academic pathways. Academic pathways have stimulated a need to rethink existing practices related to local curricular priorities and the awarding of credits. In many cases, secondary and postsecondary faculty and staff have come together to discuss ways to create more seamless transitions for students (see Chapter Three). In others, college leaders are looking at ways to improve transfer of credit. In several cases, the state has stepped in, using accountability and funding mechanisms to require agreements on policies and procedures that affect admissions, prerequisites, transfer of credits, and student support (see Chapters Four and Six). These developments are often creating changes in traditional patterns of interaction that extend well beyond specific academic pathways.

Lesson: Academic pathways are more likely to function well for students, especially underserved students, when institutions negotiate clear agreements on key transition points in the educational system. When local institutions are unable to reach such agreements, state policies may be needed to create incentives for their establishment.

Conclusion

Academic pathways are creating smoother transitions across educational levels for a range of students, including those traditionally underserved in higher education. We expect that as these pathways evolve, they will continue to play an important role in increasing access to higher education. In addition, they are contributing to changes in the configuration of the American education system, and to the ways in which students are taught and credentialed at all levels. Collaboration among education sectors will continue to spur important discussions about policy and practice, and should result in new and better ways to prepare students for the changing world.

ELISABETH A. BARNETT is senior research associate with the National Center for Restructuring Education, Schools, and Teaching at Teachers College, Columbia University, in New York, and a former APASS team member.

DEBRA D. BRAGG is professor of higher education and community college leadership, and director of the APASS initiative at the University of Illinois at Urbana-Champaign.

NEW DIRECTIONS FOR COMMUNITY COLLEGES • DOI: 10.1002/cc

INDEX

Academic pathways: career and technical education in, 73–78, 103–104; community colleges and, 6–7; conclusions on, 16–17, 107; defined, 6, 101; integrated, 102–103; multiple, 101–102; nine, 7–16; signaling role of, 31, 33, 105; student assessments and, 31–33, 105; system alignment and, 105–106

Academic Pathways to Access and Student Success (APASS), 1, 2, 6, 7–17

Adams, M., 54

Adelman, C., 22

Advanced Placement (AP) program, 8–9, 10, 103, 106

Advancement Via Individual Determination (AVID) program, 55–56

Andrews, H. A., 39

Anstrom, K., 25

Anthony, K., 75, 77

Antonio, A. L., 39

Arizona's teacher education initiative, 91, 99

Articulation models, 59, 63

Baccalaureate programs, community college: challenges of, 68–70; conclusions on, 70–71; delivery models for, 62–68; myths and realities of, 60–62; as trend, 59

Bailey, T., 8, 12, 39

Barnett, E. A., 1, 2, 3, 5, 19, 51, 53, 101, 107

Bickel, R., 40

Born, T., 2, 49, 58

Borofsky, D., 68

Boswell, K., 7, 39

Bottoms, G., 75, 77

Bottoms, J. E., 75

Bragg, D. D., 1, 2, 3, 5, 7, 16, 19, 73, 76, 81, 101, 107

Bray, J., 9

Bridge programs, 8, 9, 11

Brown, C. H., 75, 76

Bryk, A. S., 6

Bueschel, A., 2, 29, 34, 38, 105

Bush, J., 41

Cabrera, A. F., 5

California policies, 35–36

California State University Early Assessment Program (EAP), 31–33

Cameron, S. V., 14

Career and technical education (CTE), 73–78, 103–104

Carroll, C., 2, 39, 47

Chaplin, D., 14

Chen, X., 22, 23

Christensen, D., 25

College access, 5–6

College and Career Transitions Initiative (CCTI), 75, 76–77, 78, 92–99, 102, 104

College culture, shifting to, 51–52, 54–55

College Level Examination Program (CLEP), 8, 9, 11, 12

Common course numbering system, 37

Community College Baccalaureate Association (CCBA), 60, 62

Community college baccalaureate models, 59, 64, 68

Contract classes, 54, 55

Cotto, M., 63

Coxe, B., 41

Croninger, R. C., 6

Cushman, K., 25

Dare, D. E., 2, 73, 75, 76, 80

Dean, J., 63

DeLuca, S., 73

Distance learning, 8, 10, 13, 102

Distributive counseling, 53

Dodd, B. G., 12

Draeger, M. A., 2, 81, 89

Dual credit and dual enrollment, 8, 10, 12–13, 103, 106

Dual enrollment: defined, 39; in Florida, 40–42; at Lake City Community College, 43–46

Early and middle college high schools, 8, 11, 13–14

Eaton, J. S., 60, 61

Estacion, A., 73

Ewell, P., 23, 24

Faculty professional development, 86–88

Feagin, C. H., 75

Fermin, B., 12

Florida policies, 36–37

109

Back Issue/Subscription Order Form

Copy or detach and send to:

Jossey-Bass, A Wiley Imprint, 989 Market Street, San Francisco CA 94103-1741

Call or fax toll-free: Phone 888-378-2537 6:30AM – 3PM PST; Fax 888-481-2665

Back Issues: Please send me the following issues at $29 each
(Important: please include ISBN number for each issue.)

_____

_____

_____

$ _____ Total for single issues

$ _____ SHIPPING CHARGES: SURFACE   Domestic Canadian

		Domestic	Canadian
First Item		$5.00	$6.00
Each Add'l Item		$3.00	$1.50

For next-day and second-day delivery rates, call the number listed above.

Subscriptions   Please __ start __ renew my subscription to *New Directions for Community Colleges* for the year 2____ at the following rate:

U.S.	__ Individual $80	__ Institutional $195
Canada	__ Individual $80	__ Institutional $235
All Others	__ Individual $104	__ Institutional $269

Online subscriptions are available too!

**For more information about online subscriptions visit
www.interscience.wiley.com**

$ _____ Total single issues and subscriptions (Add appropriate sales tax for your state for single issue orders. No sales tax for U.S. subscriptions. Canadian residents, add GST for subscriptions and single issues.)

__Payment enclosed (U.S. check or money order only)

__VISA __ MC __ AmEx __ # _____Exp. Date _____

Signature _____ Day Phone _____
__ Bill Me (U.S. institutional orders only. Purchase order required.)

Purchase order # _____
               Federal Tax ID13559302   **GST 89102 8052**

Name _____

Address _____

_____

Phone _____ E-mail _____

For more information about Jossey-Bass, visit our Web site at www.josseybass.com

CC129 **Responding to the Challenges of Developmental Education**
Carol A. Kozeracki
Approximately 40 percent of incoming community college students enroll in developmental math, English, or reading courses. Despite the availability of popular models for teaching these classes, community colleges continue to struggle with effectively educating underprepared students, who have a wide variety of backgrounds. This volume discusses the dangers of isolating developmental education from the broader college; provides examples of successful programs; offers recommendations adaptable to different campuses; and identifies areas for future research.
ISBN: 0-7879-8050-1

CC128 **From Distance Education to E-Learning: Lessons Along the Way**
Beverly L. Bower, Kimberly P. Hardy
Correspondence, telecourses, and now e-learning: distance education continues to grow and change. This volume's authors examine what community colleges must do to make distance education successful, including meeting technology challenges, containing costs, developing campuswide systems, teaching effectively, balancing faculty workloads, managing student services, and redesigning courses for online learning. Includes case studies from colleges, plus state and regional policy perspectives.
ISBN: 0-7879-7927-9

CC127 **Serving Minority Populations**
Berta Vigil Laden
Focuses on how colleges with emerging majority enrollments of African American, Hispanic, American Indian, Asian American and Pacific Islander, and other ethnically diverse students are responding to the needs— academic, financial, and cultural—of their increasingly diverse student populations. Discusses partnerships with universities, businesses, foundations, and professional associations that can increase access, retention, and overall academic success for students of color. Covers best practices from Minority-Serving Institutions, and offers examples for mainstream community colleges.
ISBN: 0-7879-7790-X

CC126 **Developing and Implementing Assessment of Student Learning Outcomes**
Andreea M. Serban, Jack Friedlander
Colleges are under increasing pressure to produce evidence of student learning, but most assessment research focuses on four-year colleges. This volume is designed for practitioners looking for models that community colleges can apply to measuring student learning outcomes at the classroom, course, program, and institutional levels to satisfy legislative and accreditation requirements.
ISBN: 0-7879-7687-3

CC125 **Legal Issues in the Community College**
Robert C. Cloud
Community colleges must be prepared for lawsuits, federal statutes, court rulings, union negotiations, and other legal issues that could affect institutional stability and effectiveness. This volume provides leaders with information about board relations, tenure and employment, student rights and safety, disability law, risk management, copyright and technology issues, and more.
ISBN: 0-7879-7482-X

**NEW DIRECTIONS FOR COMMUNITY COLLEGES
IS NOW AVAILABLE ONLINE AT WILEY INTERSCIENCE**

What is Wiley InterScience?

Wiley InterScience is the dynamic online content service from John Wiley & Sons delivering the full text of over 300 leading scientific, technical, medical, and professional journals, plus major reference works, the acclaimed *Current Protocols* laboratory manuals, and even the full text of select Wiley print books online.

What are some special features of Wiley InterScience?

Wiley InterScience Alerts is a service that delivers table of contents via e-mail for any journal available on Wiley InterScience as soon as a new issue is published online.
Early View is Wiley's exclusive service presenting individual articles online as soon as they are ready, even before the release of the compiled print issue. These articles are complete, peer-reviewed, and citable.
CrossRef is the innovative multi-publisher reference linking system enabling readers to move seamlessly from a reference in a journal article to the cited publication, typically located on a different server and published by a different publisher.

How can I access Wiley InterScience?

Visit http://www.interscience.wiley.com

Guest Users can browse Wiley InterScience for unrestricted access to journal Tables of Contents and Article Abstracts, or use the powerful search engine. *Registered Users* are provided with a *Personal Home Page* to store and manage customized alerts, searches, and links to favorite journals and articles. Additionally, Registered Users can view free Online Sample Issues and preview selected material from major reference works.
Licensed Customers are entitled to access full-text journal articles in PDF, with select journals also offering full-text HTML.

How do I become an Authorized User?

Authorized Users are individuals authorized by a paying Customer to have access to the journals in Wiley InterScience. For example, a university that subscribes to Wiley journals is considered to be the Customer. Faculty, staff and students authorized by the university to have access to those journals in Wiley InterScience are Authorized Users. Users should contact their Library for information on which Wiley journals they have access to in Wiley InterScience.

ASK YOUR INSTITUTION ABOUT WILEY INTERSCIENCE TODAY!